Fighting WORDS

Why Government and Culture Should Fear the Church

LOUIS DAY, PHD

ISBN 978-1-0980-1272-4 (paperback)
ISBN 978-1-0980-1273-1 (digital)

Christian Faith Publishing, Inc.
832 Park Avenue
Meadville, PA 16335
www.christianfaithpublishing.com

Printed in the United States of America

CONTENTS

How to Read this

[decorative ornament]

Italicized Book Version

This book is a special, one-of-a kind *"italicized"* book:

1. If you want to get the simpler, overall call to arms of <u>Fighting Words</u>, simply <u>skip</u> the words, sentences and even paragraphs that are *italicized* within this book.
2. If you are a sceptic, doubter, or simply hunger for an in-depth perspective, read the <u>entire text</u> of <u>Fighting Words,</u> along with the *italicized* words, sentences and paragraphs.

Perhaps you are simply a "glutton for punishment". You can request your copy of my Doctoral Dissertation, <u>The Awkward Dance of Forceful Kingdoms</u> from Louis Day, <u>servantministry123@gmail.com</u>

INTRODUCTION

A Belief Worth Fighting For

"Who through faith conquered Kingdoms, enforced Justice, received promises, stopped the mouths of lions, quenched raging fire, escaped the edge of the sword, won strength out of weakness, became mighty in war, put foreign armies to flight..." (Heb. 11:33–34, RSV)

Fighting Words: Are You One of the Brave?

Are you awed, or even shocked, as you look at our culture and wonder how we got here? You completely distrust most the media; you are disgusted at what our government does and condones. Sure, you are a realist and know that there are no perfect governments nor flawless people in government, but you also know that they have weighed anchor and are floating aimlessly at sea with her citizens aboard. The symptomatic result is a culture gone wild with smatterings of violent anarchy, sexual-identity confusion, mass shootings for fame, and political figures successfully arguing for irresponsibility, entitlement, and downright unconstitutional agendas bent on destroying the Country we know, or knew.

What has happened? How did we get here? What I am about to say will probably shock you, because I doubt you have ever heard this before. What has happened? The Church. More to the point, the Church has *not* happened. The Church who was called to be a force to be reckoned with has undergone an identity crisis that has led to its emasculation. She has lost both her historical and theological moorings and has forgotten who she is and what her King's grand purpose is for her while she is in this world. She has also pulled up anchor and abandoned her responsibility to her government and has betrayed the lost masses on shore.

The resulting catastrophic devastation upon culture and nations are a symptom of her dysfunctional life style of irresponsibility. Once she saw herself, quite accurately as "a chosen race, a royal priesthood, a Holy Nation" (1 Pet. 2:9) that was called to herald God's Kingdom into the affairs of humankind. She now seems to perceive herself as a mere Bible study book club, and is content to be a mere hearer of the Word rather than a doer of transforming culture by the Word. Where she once was a force to be reckoned with that could topple Rome from the inside out, or bring the British Empire to her knees on moral issues such as slavery, she now acts more like a beaten-down slave on her government's plantation.

Once, a victorious Church could herald her champions with songs like, "Rise up O men of God, Have done with lesser things, Give heart and soul and mind and strength, to serve the King of Kings. Rise up O men of God, His Kingdom tarries long, Bring in the day of brotherhood, and end the night of wrong." If you listen to contemporary Christian music on the media or music in Church worship, you might generally get the idea that the Church is a Christian version of Woodstock rather than an army rallying its troops into action for their King. However, before you point a finger, remember, you are the Church!

Have you had enough? Are you now fighting mad? Apparently, enough of us are sufficient to elect a president of the United States who at least "tips his hat" to the Judeo-Christian God, and then some. How do we know that? The demographics of who it was that actually got Donald Trump, the forty-fifth president of the United States, into office are largely the educated, evangelical Christian.[1] Segments of America have rediscovered their bravery. Others, who had at least a moral compass to their thinking and ethics, were also largely responsible to enable a leader to begin a shocking revolution in the United States; they joined the ranks of "the land of the free, and the home of the brave." How about you? Are you one of the brave? Do you want to be?

If you are aware of the contextual background (made more and more evident in current events), President Trump had (and still has) everything going against him: the major news media, the "Deep State" powers embedded into many powerful branches of government, and the large numbers of the socialist-minded culture. Still, perhaps, you put your foot down and stood your ground with your voice and vote. Like my childhood hero, Popeye the Sailor Man, you rolled up your sleeves for a fight and said, "That's all I can stands, cuz I can't stands n'more!"

Is this how you are thinking and feeling? No matter whether you are young, old, retired or working, woman or man, no matter your racial background or party affiliation or Church denominational background, you are sick of this grotesque version of America you live in. Not only are you sick of this "zombie" version of America trying to take over, you are mad enough to "rise up…to have done with lesser things," you are ready to "give heart and soul and mind and strength, to serve the King of Kings. Rise up O people of God, bring in the day of brotherhood, and end the night of wrong." Yes? Then welcome to the heart of God, welcome to the honorable brotherhood and sisterhood of fellow warriors who are called by God to fulfill a mission long abandoned by Churchianity!

How dare I passionately proclaim such a call to arms? By what authority do I, or do you, take this disposition toward our culture and government? This author is known to be a conservative Christian theologian and a postgraduate Biblical exegete with credentials in the Biblical languages. My conviction and passion were set on fire by being a student of the Scriptures, Church history, American history, and the Constitution of the United States, all of which culminated into my PhD dissertation. The above mentioned are not meant to be braggadocios. It is intended to let the reader know that my discovery of the passion and heart of God in these realms come from a thorough examination into the Scriptures with judicious application into our contemporary situation. The Bible has informed my politics, not the other way around!

You will see that we are not alone in our passion to see our culture and Country transformed back to its sane heritage. You will find that you are in camaraderie of fellow citizens who are a force to be reckoned with. You will discover, as I did, there are leaders out there who share our informed passion. Even a Baptist theologian and national leader will call you to join the fight by declaring, "The Kingdom of God is a declaration of war!"[2]

Quotations from the Scriptures are from the New American Standard Bible (NASB), unless stated otherwise.

CHAPTER 1

Reasons behind the Fight

You've heard it before. Break down the word *assume*, it will make an "ass" out of "u" and "me." Although meant to be humorous, there's a lot of truth behind that saying. As a certified firearms instructor, I also teach mass shooter event confrontation training for schools, hospitals, businesses, and Churches. I have seen firsthand how important it is for my students to leave incorrect assumptions behind the door of my class and at the entrance of the shooting range so that they may be correctly trained and informed.

The same is true of you. We all have assumptions and presuppositions behind everything we believe in. Before we ever engage in any serious endeavor, we need to check our assumptions, our presuppositions and examine if they are true—to see if they are true and strong enough to fight for, or even die for. You must discover your "why" to fight.

Allow me to guide you through some key areas about the Bible, Christianity, Church, self-defense, government, and other areas in which, like me, you've probably held to some false assumptions. Based upon much scholastic and historical research, this call to a Biblical revolution, your call to "fight the good fight" is based upon some critical, accurate presuppositions we will use so that you become a man, a woman who will change history for now and eternity. I will call these tested assumptions *critical building blocks*.

Critical Building Block 1: God's Heart Is More than Just "Getting People Saved"

You would think that if you opened the Bible, you will see all God cares about is eternal salvation and evangelism and He only passingly tips His hat to this world and societal problems. Where one does spend eternity is of paramount importance! However, that dimension is only part of what God cares about in our world. He also cares deeply about the lonely orphan, the abused wife, the suicidal teen, the forgotten and the marginalized, and those who weep themselves to sleep with hunger. He cares about economics and the environment, within its proper perspective.

You have but to read the Gospels—Matthew, Mark, Luke, and John—to catch a glimpse of Jesus's heart for the hurting and of His rage against inJustice in culture. He is passionate about the health of society, governments that reward the good actions and punish the bad deeds. God's grace includes His forgiveness for wrongs against Him and the feeding of the hungry. He cares about a judicial system based upon His Justice. He hates a system of government that places a young man in prison who stole a case of beer from his neighbor's garage for the same length of time as a murderer. He longs to see legal systems based upon the "rule of law"—that is, His Law and not mere laws made up by human beings.

What about you? Do you share in these same ideals? Do you wish for the same? If so, you are reflecting the "image of God" He has stamped in you, and at best, you are reflecting the heart of your Father. He wants His Kingdom to come, His will be done on earth, even as it is in heaven.

The phrase "the Kingdom of God" is so misunderstood and abused. However both of these dimensions, one's eternal state and society's immediate health are included in that phrase and reality. It was God's idea to create government. He cares about governments. He also clearly dictates that He rules over it and that those in government will answer to Him.

Let's look at how God sees the world. If not obvious to any sane person, the Scriptures tell us that "sin," the major dysfunction of writing God out of life, has affected the entire world. Just as we have individually sinned, so have we corporately sinned from a community to a national and global level as well. Look around you and read your daily media, and you will find that your stomach churns, your heart sickens. Sometimes you just weep when you read certain stories of evil all around you.

Equally true though, is that the redemption and grace of God that has affected the individual and the Church for all eternity is also intended to affect all this temporary world and culture around us! God too sickens at the evil around us, and wants us to remedy much of it with Him. The "Kingdom of God" is not some lofty idea for the "sweet bye and bye," and it certainly isn't about some cultish shaved-head fanatics hiding out in some compound planning to take over the world with bad Kool-Aid. It is about God's desire for a healthy society in which the orphan is loved and cared for, all humans are esteemed, poverty is scarce, and streets are safe. It is His will that government serves the people and when certain officials don't, they are thrown out of office immediately by His Rule of Law, and people are freed up to be their very best.

It is about seeing a black community gathering arm-in-arm around mostly white police officers and praying for them for their protection before they go to work. It is about a sixty hour a week waitressing, single mother falling to her knees weeping when she gets a $1,000 tip to care for her children.

When people catch a glimpse of this kind of God reflected by His representatives, they will more easily believe and trust Him for their eternal care. However imperfectly fleshed out this side of heaven, God's Kingdom, with His people, are to be a transformational force in this world for God's glory. That's exactly how slavery ended in England and the United States! Throughout history, where do most hospitals, orphanages, and higher schools of learning come from? As will be described later, this is the "temporal" or "cultural" mandate from God in distinction from His eternal mandate.

The salvation of people by God, and collectively known as the "Church" (another greatly abused and misunderstood word), are also meant to be a temporal yet penetrating redemption of society and nations. Our growth in God's grace is to be a seasoning for the earth:

"You are the salt of the earth" (Matt.5:13). Our liberty in Christ is meant for us to be lights of His Justice: "You are the light of the world...Let your light shine before men in such a way as they may see your good works, and glorify your Father who is in heaven" (Matt. 5:14, 16).

This sense of the triumphant Church heralding God's kingdom drove God's people to build a nation (the United States, in particular) to produce universities (Harvard and Yale, as historically stellar examples) to abolish slavery on two continents, and to build orphanages and countless hospitals, just to list a few samples within Church history. I argue that the Church's purpose is much more than just being a narcissistic, apathetic Body only concerned with its own health and growth. Rather, the Biblical view is that the people of God are a force to be reckoned with. Its very existence is bent as an offensive force in the world to glorify God in every dimension upon earth whether it be the legal system, the arts, education, government and politics, or the helping of the poor.

Yes, on the one hand, we are to seek to persuade people to Christ and to introduce them to His eternal salvation. Equally true, we are to introduce Christ the King to all of humankind and to persuade them back to Eden. This is not an either/or work of God through us; rather it is a both/and mandate from God. It does no good to separate these two—the salvation of people and the salvation of culture—into two camps, as God Himself does not. To do so would be just as erroneous as to split apart "make disciples of all men" (Matt. 25:19) from "Let you light shine before all men" (Matt.5:16). I am not abandoning my evangelical roots or the importance of where one spends eternity. Nor is my passion a "social gospel" argument either, where all that matters is taking up social causes. The eternal salvation of people, bringing them into God's Kingdom through faith in Christ alone, is not being compromised nor minimized in the least. *Rather,* I hope to revive the neglected cultural, temporal mandate of God's heart and mind. When we examine the Gospels of Jesus Christ, who was (and is) "very God" and "very man" while He existed in our time and space real world, we find He consistently accomplished both. His "The Kingdom of God is at hand" proclamation not only called people to eternal salvation, it transformed both Jewish culture and the Roman Empire.

"Salvation," in this way, is meant to permeate the world around us. All societies and all governments around the world are under the authority of Christ and His Kingdom, regardless of whether they acknowledge it or not. Jesus declared in Matthew 28:18, "Given to me all authority in both heavens and upon earth" (my personal translation from the Greek text). Christ's kingship is not just a mere theory to be entertainingly preached about from a pulpit or comfortably outlined in a Sunday school classroom; it is an actual reality that permeates His creation.

Christ's rule is not just upon mere earth; it extends to the entire cosmos and "...the visible and invisible, whatever thrones or lordships, whatever government offices or authorities, all of it was created by His means and for His purposes" (Col. 1:16, my personal translation). It is our mission to recognize and promote His rule. God's people need to be bold and to practice this reality by actions and proclamation to all society, which includes government and her officials. A Southern Baptist leader wrote, "The Kingdom's advance is set in motion by the Galilean march out of the graveyard. We should then be the last people to skulk back in fear or apathy...we do not despair as those who are the losers in history might. We are the future kings and queens of the universe."[1] We are not called to be "losers in history"; we are on the King's mission to be history makers.

We are accustomed to hearing Churches teach the eternal mandate from Christ that we are to seek to persuade men and women to Christ and to introduce them to His eternal salvation. However, another clear command appears very much dismissed: we are also to introduce Christ the King to all humankind and persuade them to His Truth and His Law, that His operating manual for this world brings wholeness and good to people and society.

There's an old joke that asks the question, "Do you know the difference between apathy and ignorance?" One waits for the awkward pause and mockingly answers their own question, "I don't know and I don't care!" As citizens of God's Kingdom, we are called to neither apathy nor ignorance but to a revolutionary advancement of His kingship and His rule over all, and that means to seek to have His Law as a basis for all humankind. This is a compassionate, loving movement to be involved in. It will be from this clear but vastly ignored call of God upon His people to advance His kingship that we will now proceed to understand what His "Law" looks like. If you call yourself a Christian or believer but seem hesitant about God's citizens speaking to government and politics, I humorously quote Archbishop Desmond Tutu, "Who's to say religion and politics don't mix? Whose Bible are they reading anyway?"[2]

Critical Building Block 2: Who Draws the Fighting Line in the Sand over Law, Use of Force, and Our US Constitution?

Now this may sound like a boring topic, but I guarantee that it is not! If you read and process the following truth from Scripture, it may mean the difference between your choice to either obey a Law or to choose to disobey it! Your personal compass will be magnetized into your conscience, making you into a warrior for "right and wrong," and you will join the legacy of world changers. You will understand to your core that you answer to God first and secondly to any other level of government.

Fair warning! You may now find yourself in a life-transforming journey, should you continue. Are you willing? Are you ready? Yes? Then we must begin by asking the following questions: What exactly is law? Who defines what Law is? Who are the caretakers of law? You? Me? Judges? Law enforcement? Our hirelings in public office? Furthermore, how does our Constitution of the United States relate to God and His law?

In turn, you may ask, "How does this 'eye-opening revelation' practically fit into our everyday lives?" Hopefully these questions will be answered and you will wonder why you have not heard much about this from your Church. Most of these Biblical discussions are reserved for theological elites, or your Church leaders, but are not entrusted to the common people, which includes most pastors and clergy. In fact, most Church leaders have never been even introduced and challenged to such Biblical discussions. That is a huge shame! You can change that right at your home base.

As we will see, as Christians, we are all, without exception of age or race, called as ambassadors to the world, including to our governments. Christians hold a dual citizenship; one to our earthly country and her government and one to our heavenly King who rules over both. In particular, to you Christians who are reading this book and who are citizens of the United States with that dual citizenship, you are compelled to ask a pertinent question about our citizenry and its history. At the time of our government's creation, what was the backdrop of the Bible and its relationship to our Declaration of Independence and our Constitution?

Here's the clincher! Because this discussion of Church and State relationships includes both the question of authority and the God-given use of force by each, all Christians, no matter what their worldly citizenship is, must answer the question of the Biblical view of the use of force. I have had to answer what the Biblical conclusions were about pacifism versus activism, as do you. As you read and contemplate these Biblical issues, you are compelled to ask how your conclusions play out in both your private responsibilities (self-defense, of others and of property) and your public responsibility (police and military). You will find yourself asking how these conclusions might lead you into a "just war" theory and make you rethink your government's acts of war or your police force actions.

Please do not get me wrong here. Any military or police personnel know me to be supportive and respectful of their sacrificial service. However, you will find a strong Biblical grid with which to analyze their actions as just or unjust. The rest of this first chapter is meant to briefly explore and explain these questions and to shed light behind the larger questions of Church and State relationships. I remind you that we cannot fully develop these topics, but hope to introduce you into some revolutionary thinking greatly ignored in your Church and family circle discussions.

Where Does the Idea of "Law" Come From?

You may have never thought about this, but hang in here, it is an eye-opening thought process that will change your thinking! There are only two possibilities as to where law, or an absolute of "right and wrong," Justice and inJustice, "good or bad" can come from. One which starts exclusively from this material realm, (the universe and man within a "box") or, alternately, that which starts from a "transcendent" (meaning, outside, above and beyond and not dependent on the "box") Creator and Lawgiver, Who is outside of this material realm.

These two definitions of reality stand strictly opposed to each other and cannot be logically, theologically, philosophically, and, therefore, never legally, combined together. God's people, and many others, simply assume the second worldview through intellectual investigation or simple assumption. This transcendent "outside the box" God has chosen to make himself known to us through acts history and in the Scriptures, known as "revelation." From this second worldview comes the nature and basis of "Law" that is outside of and above humanity in authority. In other words, humankind is not the source of Law, God is.

However, in order to clarify this God-centered worldview, one must look at the alternate worldview first and its lack of basis for "law." So much of what you see in Congress or in courts has no basis for "Law" whatsoever. Let us start with the "in the box" view; what you will see to be an insane basis for Law.

The Insane View: The Physical World Defines Everything (Materialism)

If one begins with the premise that this material realm is all there really is and all that ever will be, that means that the material realm alone defines what reality is. Therefore, there cannot be a Creator, no external Law Giver, and no Transcendent Person outside of the material. Morality, ethics, and definitions of right, wrong, Justice, and, therefore, freedom *must be defined from within that realm of within the material universe only.*

As Dr. Dale Tackett from the "Truth Project" best illustrates this basis for reality, one has to look for answers and foundations only within the "box" of the material realm; there is nothing outside of the "box."[3] Therefore, humans can define what "law" is. Think about this: "law" becomes whatever the whims of an individual or groups of individuals at any given point in time locked into their "box." The order of society, government, and Law will fluctuate and wane with whatever humans decide at their time and place in history. We can redefine marriage. We can come up with whatever economic system we want. We can make up what a country or constitution should be, dictatorial or anarchy. We alone will determine what is right, good, or bad. At best, a majority rules, at worst, the guys with the most guns rule. Hitler decides what is right. His Law is law, and that goes for any dictator, group of individuals, or a serial killer.

This worldview cannot tolerate any other view. For example, the US Constitution is clearly based upon the transcendent worldview (just read it and note this clear assumption within both the Declaration and Constitution). *However, Supreme Court Chief Justice Charles Evan Hughes would defy the transcendent worldview and boldly announce, from his "in the box" worldview, "…the Constitution is what the judges say it is"[4] in his attempt to force it into a "boxed in" materialistic worldview. The Supreme Court, he says, can decide what Law is, whatever they decide. There is, therefore, no one outside of this world or universe to inform humanity of what Law is and should be. Humanity has no intrinsic value, and the paradigmatic "Might makes right" will prevail, whether that "might" be violent force or political elections.*

Reflecting the same man-centered pomposity, a 1936 decree of the Third Reich Commissar of Justice mandated, "A decision of the Fuhrer in the express form of Law or decree may not be scrutinized by a judge."[5] This goes back to *Rex Lex*, the king is law. Do you see where this worldview ends up? Hitler, who has the most guns (and tanks and planes and soldiers), says Jews are not human and should be exterminated like cockroaches; that's his "law." Therefore, his Law is right. The basis of Law is limited only to humanity's limited, finite experience within the box of the material universe. The concept of Law is trapped within the cosmos medium. Who are you, or anybody else, to say that Hitler was wrong? You have no right to say so, unless it is by more guns than he had. Then you can dictate your "law" over everybody else.

Within this perception, there can be no absolutes, no basis for Law in the materialistic, anthropocentric worldview. This is the current state of our culture at large and education system. No one can ultimately decide what is "wrong" or "right." I ask again, what right does anyone have to judge Adolf Hitler for his genocidal actions? He made the Law to do so and judged it right. Who is to say otherwise?

What is our conclusion to such ludicrousy? The Biblical statement of this world view is clear: "Professing to be wise they became fools...For they exchanged the truth of God for a lie, and worshipped and served the creature rather than the Creator" (Rom 1:22, 25). *The word for creature here is, "ktisei," or "creation, created order"; something "within the box." The insanity of this position is made clear by this passage; God, the eternal, infinite Creator is "dead." Now man and nature have claims to deity!* However, let's turn the page to a more sane, realistic, and logical worldview.

The Sane View: God Himself Defines Everything (Transcendent Law)

This can be simplified as the worldview that says, "There is a God, and we are not Him." *As opposed to materialistic-anthropocentric worldview is the (watch out, here it comes!) Judeo/Christian Theocentric/ Transcendent worldview. These big words simply describe a worldview where God is above and beyond the material, created order.* He has chosen to reveal himself by communicating to us who he is, and acts and speaks within this material world to inform us of His "Owner's Manual" for our world. Jesus stated, "My Kingdom is not of this world" (John 18:36).

The original Greek text points to the fact that Christ's Kingdom is not "derived from" or "sourced from" this world. What Jesus was telling Pilate was that His Kingdom and His Law are transcendent and above this world. His Kingdom rule of Law stands above man's law, and is to inform man's law. Because God, the Creator, made the cosmos, and is therefore the Law Giver, He sets absolutes that are not up to opinions or votes.

These absolutes are also within reach humankind's understanding; there is a system to give order to society. *Because God revealed Himself in the Bible, "It provides a tangible standard whereby Justice can be obtained. The Law system that has its reference point in the Bible works because it conforms to truth and the way in which the world really functions."*[6] God, the reality maker, has given to us the standard operating procedures for the universe and humankind.

Who then Defines What "Law" Is?

Can you see the insanity of the first worldview? *You can now see that the Judeo-Christian presupposition that Law necessarily derives from the Transcendent Creator-Lawgiver; He and His nature define it above all. The question can be asked if our presupposition behind "law" has valid, logical reasoning behind it.* Please remember, Christianity is based upon faith but that faith is based upon evidence and facts; it is testable by the scrutiny of historical evidence and logical conclusions. Based upon this worldview, all laws derive from a higher principle, and "any legal system, secular or otherwise, must develop a religious foundation of law, and maintain that foundation by hostility to any other Law order or it will falter."[7]

If you are looking to diagnose why there is such hostility in culture clashes and government strife, this is it. For the Materialist, ultimately, whether they admit it or not, the cosmos is that which they worship; it is their "religious" center and base. They are neither humanitarian nor logical fanatics when they act out; they are their own brand of religious fanatics. These "fanatics" can go about redefining marriage and family, as well as sexual identities. They can legalize execution of innocent children within a mother's nurturing womb. They can choose to rewrite history to eradicate any reality that disturbs their private worldview.

For the Christian throughout time and globally, and for the Christian within the historical context of the United States, our "religious foundation of law" is God's character as revealed in Scripture. Who will define Law, eternal God, or finite man from conclusions within a finite box? Long before the United States existed, Blackstone (who was a premier jurist in England and who heavily influenced the theory of Law in the United States) made no apologies for that Judeo-Christian basis for Law, and who it is that defines Law: *"The doctrines thus delivered we call the revealed or divine law, and they are to be found only in the Holy Scriptures. Upon these two foundations, the Law of nature and the Law of revelation depend all human laws; that is to say, no human laws should be suffered to contradict these."*[8] *Up until recently, every attorney studying for a Law degree had Blackstone's commentaries as a requirement for their library. Ask your attorney if he or she remembers that, or if they even know who he was. If not, find another attorney.*

Within the Judeo-Christian atmosphere of the American colonies, Blackstone's contribution to English common law, which used Biblical principles in judicial decisions, found its way into the colonial documents (the Declaration of Independence and the United States Constitution). It is not mere coincidence that the phrase "Laws of Nature and Nature's God" find their way into the Declaration through Blackstone, though paraphrased by Jefferson. In Biblical revelation, the American founders discovered that a "system of absolutes exists upon which government and Law can be founded."[9] The foundational base from which to derive and define laws of men was "God's written Law, back through the New Testament to Moses' written Law; and the content and authority of that written Law is rooted back to Him who is the final reality."[10]

You will not read or hear the following in current education and media: such was the common understanding of a government under the Law of God that even before the Revolutionary War had ended, there was a paid chaplain in Congress and all thirteen colonies in their provincial congresses opened with prayer. It continued even after the national Congress formed. They knew they were building the government and her laws upon the Creator God revealed in the Judeo-Christian Scriptures. That presuppositional foundation for Law continued in the United States throughout her history.

Consider the following: As recently as 1978, Kentucky mandated that the Ten Commandments be posted in its public classrooms with the following explanation attached, "The secular application of the Ten Commandments is clearly seen in its adoption as the fundamental legal code of Western civilization and the Common Law of the United States."[11] Why don't we hear about these evidences today? It is because our government and culture fear the Church and its history as a formidable force!

Let's clear up a common misunderstanding: The Biblical application and definition of Law does not mean a Theocratic form of government, as is falsely alleged by many. Know this distinction: a theocracy is a government that seeks God's direct, immediate guidance, much like Israel's earliest years in the Old Testament through her prophets. In contrast, within the New Testament, God's Kingdom citizens are admonished to "be in subjection to the governing authorities" (Rom. 12:1) and to "Submit yourselves for the Lord's sake to every human institution" (1 Pet. 2:13). Those commands take place in the historical setting of an Imperial Roman government. As we will investigate the question, "Who administers law?" it is found that the Judeo-Christian paradigm, informed by theology, is to have God's Law applied and mediated through faulty, fallen human governments.

Even within that paradigm, conflict can, and should, arise at times between God's Kingdom and man's Kingdom. This is the divine tension and conflict between kingdoms. When government is told by God's Kingdom citizen who it is that defines law, conflict can, and does arise. Even looking back to the early formation of the Church, we see the tension fomenting: "Herod feared Christ because He represented a Kingdom greater than his own. Christians were martyred not for religious reasons but because they would not say, 'We have no king but Caesar', the Roman government saw them as political subversives."[12] Who it is that defines law, God or man, is critical to the results within society and the world.

Who then Should Be the Umpire Over Laws?

Remember, as we answer this question of who umpires over legitimate Law or illegitimate law, we return to the Original Creator of Law, just as the early American forefathers did in setting forth our Country's legal system of government. This is known as, "administration of law." Some of what we are about to discover and think through may be refreshing logically, or challenging, or both.

Although the Church does have the revealed Word of God in the Scriptures, Church history will reveal that she may take decades, or even centuries, to refine certain important doctrines, particularly those which must be applied to different cultures and times throughout history. This is the case for the significant application of the doctrine of Church and State relationships. How do we take the Scriptural discussions of government and culture, and then apply them to the present government and culture of today?

Do the Biblical applications apply to ANTIFA, the Deep State within the present legitimate state, and the Republican and Democratic platforms? Does the Bible speak directly to our current foreign relations, who our police and military are and how they are to act and what welfare and jobs should look like? *The present understanding of who administers Law did not develop significantly until the Reformation. Franky Schaeffer observes that both Luther and Calvin, without even realizing it at the time, laid the philosophical foundation for Law and government, which eventually led to the American Revolution.*[13] Now this is critically important for you, the reader, as an investigator; what you study in the Scriptures, and how God ignites your inward fire in wanting to see God's Law and Justice applied may find you forming history!

The Protestant Reformation was a schism in Western Christianity initiated by Martin Luther and continued by John Calvin, Huldrych Zwingli, and other Protestant Reformers in sixteenth-century Europe. What is important to note is that the Reformers who had so much to do with our present Biblical view of God's Law were not anarchists, or against government. They knew well the Biblical injunctions to submit to governing authorities. For example, John Calvin argued, "Paul enjoins obedience toward the magistrate, not only for fear of punishment, but for conscience' sake [Rom. 13:1, 5]. From this it follows that consciences are also bound by civil laws."[14]

The great clash of the Reformers was over the relationship of government under God and government's proper administration of Law. They had long experienced abuse and misunderstanding on this concept. They were in a petri dish in time to work through a Biblical view of God and government.

Today we are at the same critical juncture. Just think, how often are you simply "ticked off" because your government seems to be clueless about Justice or morality? From seeing the previous distinctive worldviews, you will then understand why the Reformation simply claimed that governing authorities were under God's Law, just like the people they ruled. Whether you are the president of the United States or a blue-collar worker, the Law equally applies. The milieu of the Reformation era was that monarchies and other governing authorities would claim "*Rex Lex*"; the "king is law." Therefore, the king makes and dispenses Law as he will (a form of anthropocentric-deity law; Law within the "box").

By contrast, the Biblical view was, and is, and ever will be, "*Lex Rex*"; "(God's) Law is king." All humanity, king and peasant, are to bow to that unchangeable Law. *The overall outcome of this debate and battle during this period was that the basis of Law and its administration did not stem from the Church alone, but from Scripture itself as the final authority, or "Sola Scriptura"[15]* In other words, both the State and the Church, as separate institutions ordained by God, are both under God's rule of Law as revealed in the Scriptures. God, who created the Church and government, rules over both. God is the ultimate Umpire, the rightful Administrator over both!

This reality does not deny the State its God-given authority. *Bonhoeffer flatly declares about the State institution, "In its being, it is a divine office,"[16] thereby reflecting the apostle Paul's inspired declaration, "Those which exist (governing authorities) are established by God" and "whoever resists authority has opposed the ordinance of God" (Rom. 13:1–2). Humankind did not invent the idea of government, God did!* It is God's intention that fallen human governments bring about Justice and order in this fallen world and, as such, bear the authority of God.

The form the state takes, although important, takes secondary import to this clear doctrine,[17] *or as Calvin had said earlier,* "Obviously, it would be an idle pastime for men…to dispute over what would be the best kind of government in that place where they live. The nature of the discussion depends largely upon the circumstances."[18] However, as United States citizens, we believe the early founders' "American experiment" of a limited government with checks and balances is a formidable attempt at balancing state and Church powers, and is taken from a Biblical model.

From the Scriptures, we know that God expects government to administer Law faithfully as "ministers of God" (Rom. 13:1); government is to derive its laws for order and morality from God's Law, not make them up "willy-nilly." As citizens, our expectations of government should be no less than God's own expectations of government. Particular laws that the State administers and enforces within its governance are to be derived from God's Law.[19] As Whitehead will put it, the classic principle and rule of thumb for lawmaking is "Law is found, not made."[20] For example, speed limits on the highways are based upon "Thou shalt not steal" (destruction of another's property by an accident) and "Thou shalt not kill" (the careless destruction of life by an accident). Vehicles have the potential to be deadly weapons or destructive devices. Speed limits are a "found" Law based on His Law concerning theft and murder.

Here are some good definitions of law. The Latin legal term legisprudence *answers the question of "What is legal?" (as defined by the state, right or wrong). The legal term* jurisprudence *seeks to answer the question "What is just?" (as defined by the Creator). The American founders knew and discussed this philosophy of Law as based upon God's Scriptural and natural revelation. We are to expect our government to seek jurisprudence before seeking legisprudence. Whitehead examined the derivation of the phrase "the Laws of Nature and Nature's God" within the Declaration of independence and perceived it as a precedence of jurisprudence, not legisprudence.*[21] *Jurisprudence is the standard for all law. It would be for reason of King George's lack of jurisprudence, the lack of faithful administration of Law under God, which the American colonies would revolt against and claim independence. If you are a citizen of the United States, you are so because of a people who called out their government (King George, who thought he could make up law) to follow jurisprudence.*

It is quite clear that human governments are comprised of fallen and sinful human beings ("for all have sinned and fall short of the glory of God," Rom. 3:23) yet are established by God to bring Justice and order to society (Rom. 13:1; 1 Pet. 2:13–14). Please read the following carefully: It is the Church's responsibility to be the "salt and light" (Matt. 5:13–16) to her culture, including her governments. Within the New Testament alone, we see John the Baptist opposing Governor Herod's morality, Jesus's prophetic word against rulers and leaders that offended them greatly, the Apostles taking a stand for Christ and against religion-political leaders in the Book of Acts, and so forth.

An important Biblical and historical note here is that Jesus, His Apostles, and most of the early Church were killed as enemies of the state—governmental threats, as the State saw it. For the most part, the blind culture supported their actions. Both government's administrations of Law under God and the Church's responsibility to hold government accountable to God's Law are God's revealed will. Both cause a divine tension, an awkward dance, which is forever being refined. Government is to administer her laws, but her definitions and limits are under the scrutiny of God's Law, and His people are to hold that government and her leaders accountable to that rule of Law.

How well do you think we are doing right now in the United States? How well are you and your Church doing as God's ambassadors and representatives to our government and culture? A contemporary theologian and pastor, well-respected throughout the world, spoke unapologetically:

> The civil government, as all of life, stands under the Law of God. In this fallen world, God has given us certain offices to protect us from the chaos that is the natural result of that fallenness.

27

> But when *any office* commands that which is con-
> trary to the Word of God, those who hold that
> office abrogate their authority and they are not to
> be obeyed. And that includes the state.[22]

Let me draw the bottom line: It is God who defines Law and, consequently, what Justice is and what Righteousness and morality mean from His absolute standards. Humankind is to discover Law from God's revealed Word. God has ordained that government exist and is to administer Law, but they are to derive laws applicable to its governing of people righteously. Law is found by man, not made by man. Furthermore, government stands under God's Law, neither above it nor beside it, and any political leader abrogates its authority whenever it "creates" laws that are contrary to God's Law. Therefore, we, God's people, have the responsibility under our King to get out to the dance floor and have that awkward dance of forceful Kingdoms.

Our Unique Constitution

Created by Using a Biblical Map and Compass

As I was writing the first chapter of my doctoral dissertation before this book, it was July 1, 2016, three days from the United States' Independence Day celebration. I had just read these words from John Adams to his wife, dated July 3, 1776:

> The second day of July, 1776 will be the most
> memorable epoch in the history of America. I am
> apt to believe that it will be celebrated by suc-
> ceeding generations as the great anniversary fes-
> tival. It ought to be commemorated as the day of
> deliverance, by solemn acts of devotion to God
> Almighty. It ought to be solemnized with pomp
> and parade, with shows, games, sports, guns,
> bonfires, and illuminations, from one end of the

continent to the other, from this time forward
forever more.[23]

The cultural environment of the times of the Revolution, and
the formation of the United States by its essential documents, the
Declaration of Independence, and the Unites States Constitution,
was a thoroughly Biblical one; it was the "map" of the times. It is an
absolute denial of the historical records and an absolute lie to deny
this hard fact. That is not to say that other, more secular ideas stemming from the Enlightenment were present also.

However, as a case in point to the overwhelming Biblical environment in this Country's formative years. My ancestor Benjamin
Franklin, in Pennsylvania, June 28, 1787, thought to be one of
the least religious patriot fathers (and even scandalous in his ethical behavior at times, as records reveal), stated in a speech to the
Constitutional Convention,

> All of us who were engaged in the struggle must
> have observed frequent instances of superintend-
> ing providence in our favor. To that kind prov-
> idence we owe this happy opportunity of con-
> sulting in peace on the means of establishing our
> future national felicity. And have we now forgot-
> ten that powerful friend? Or do we imagine that
> we no longer need his assistance? I have lived,
> Sir, a long time, and the longer I live, the more
> convincing proofs I see of this truth-that God
> governs in the affairs of men. And if a sparrow
> cannot fall to the Ground without his Notice, is
> it probable that an Empire can rise without his
> Aid? I therefore beg leave to move—that hence-
> forth prayers imploring the assistance of Heaven,
> and its blessings on our deliberations, be held in
> this Assembly every morning before we proceed
> to business, and that one or more of the Clergy of
> this City be requested to officiate in that service.[24]

How does the above speech sound to you in our current gross misrepresentation of "separation of Church and state"? One can ask, of whom was Adams referring to when he wrote "God Almighty" in his letter to his wife? Of whom and of what record was Franklin referring when he spoke of a "sparrow falling to the ground without his notice" if not the Gospels of the New Testament?

Historians have long documented this Biblical map of early America. C. Gregg Singer observed, "A Christian world and life view furnished the basis for this early political thought which guided the American people for nearly two centuries and who's crowning lay in the writing of the Constitution in 1787." As well, Alexis de Tocqueville remarked, "America is still the place where the Christian religion has kept the greatest real power over men's souls" [25]

Are you reading or hearing this today? Of course not! Why not? Because our government and culture no longer fear the Church as a formidable force contrary to their worldview and agenda! They have apparently succeeded in putting you and the Church in our "proper place" of silence and submission!

A flood of quotes from the American founders and a hurricane of documents from historians well establish the Biblical map of the American Constitutional times. This does not mean that the "Biblical compass" of that historical setting would translate into our contemporary "evangelical Christianity" of today. The culture was simply that from the common person to the American public official, a Biblical knowledge of God and theological worldview were much more prevalent, pervasive and in effect than in today's American society. That Biblical map would set the foundations for the Biblical compass for our nation, and is the basis for which our Country has been so blessed.

The Biblical Compass Guiding our Constitution

A quick recounting of the history behind the Biblical compass of the American colonies is in order. In Europe, during the seventeenth century, the political context was a governmental system that held to the divine

*right of kings. What the king did and said, loosely speaking, was "law,"
encapsulated in the Latin phrase "Rex Lex" or, "the king is law." Samuel
Rutherford, a renowned Presbyterian minister would send shockwaves
throughout the world and in history in his historical book* Lex Rex, *or
the Law and the Prince. The mirror image of the phrase "Rex Lex" into
"Lex Rex," or "Law is king," was, and is a historical milestone and the
"true North" of governmental affairs. His basic theological-legal argument was that the king (and government officials) was under law, God's
Law, and accountable to the citizens for being so.*

*His premise of a government based upon Biblical principles would
echo into the hearts of William Blackstone, John Witherspoon, and John
Locke, all of whom would greatly affect the formation of American history.*[26] *Our Founding fathers knew how worldviews directed government
and they favored the Judeo-Christian one over others. Even a semi-Deist
like Thomas Jefferson would take John Locke's version of Lex Rex and
produce a secularized version of it as his paradigm for government,*[27]
which would frame our government's Constitution.

*Blackstone was an eighteenth-century lecturer on Law at Oxford.
His* Commentaries on the Laws of England *(1765–1770), based upon
Judeo-Christian theism, became the premiere textbook on law, not only
in England but also in America. Thomas Jefferson knew from his legal
perspicuity that the state itself could not give men "inalienable rights" but
that only one, the Creator alone, could do so.*[28]

*One of the principle reasons by which one can logically establish the
American society's Biblical solidarity is through rightly defining the terms
and concepts used within the Declaration and Constitution. Negligence
of the Biblical context and consensus of the times can lead to gross misunderstanding or manipulation of those documents.*

*Larry Arnn cites an example where the "Speaker of the House Nancy
Pelosi will mock the Constitution on the one hand and yet revere the
Declaration on the other. Just as the Speaker abandons the Constitution,
so she alters the meaning of the Declaration. Nor is she alone."*[29]

*Please hear the following closely: Whether or not Speaker Pelosi (or
any other politician) knows the historical context, Biblical milieu and
consensus of the time, or whether or not she even understands the import
of the meaning of words to legal documents, is secondary.* What is crit-

ical is that we, God's people, God's agents of His Kingdom, are to be aware of these facts and to think and decisively act upon them, just as the early colonists did. We were handed a map and compass by our King; it is imperative to know how to use them! Upon the legal foundation of Blackstone, who said the "will of the Maker is called the Law of nature" and the Biblical-legal cornerstone of *Lex Rex*, these passionate colonists would ensure that "all men are created equal" and, "Nature and Nature's God" would find its way into their national documents.

We enjoy so many freedoms in our Country because of these Biblical ideas structured within our documents, and it is our duty to hold government accountable for them. We are to demand that they use our historical compass and map and not lead our Country blindly through perilous territory! The Biblical compass became the colonist's rationale and platform for legal independence from a king who saw himself above God's Law, and the creator of Law at his own whim (*Rex Lex*).

"The colonists argued that it is "the Laws of Nature and Nature's God" that entitled them to independence and to an equal station among nations."[30] However, in defiance or ignorance of this historical setting of the early founders, within our education system and media, we observe an intentional historical revisionism and rewriting of historical documents. The result is that "'Nature' in Jefferson's sense has been replaced with an evolutionary process (of our Constitution)-clarification mine)."[31] The practical implication is that in their worldview, there are no absolutes from which to base morality and law.

Here are some "fighting words" based upon these fighting truths: Those who would impose such deceit upon others should be called to truth and honesty, and God's people are called to do precisely that as citizens of God's Kingdom. God expects we, His people to lead the fight for "we, the people," and "we, the people" are called to fight!

One other consideration on Constitutional building blocks is highlighted by a brief history of "Common Law." The Courts of England had her roots in a Biblical Law from which principles of Law among men were derived. This derivation of legal principles was known as "Common

Law." Common Law described the Law common between men and God. Common Law was established in the English courts and would eventually find its way into verbiage of the Constitution. In fact, the Seventh Amendment to the Constitution makes reference to this common Law as ruling over other laws as the "higher law."

This Biblical derivation of Common Law simply corroborates the theological DNA inherent to the founder's worldview and into the courts of American law. An argument that the phrase "common law" is vague simply lacks historical veracity and legal integrity; it is deception and a lie. Joseph Story, professor of Law at Harvard University, clarified this twisting of truth by stating, "There never has been a period in which Common Law did not recognize Christianity as laying its foundation."[32] Common Law has as its jurisprudential spine, Biblical Law. Whether educated or not, it is idiocy to deny this reality.

The foundational presuppositions behind the Constitution are primarily Biblical theology and Christian philosophy. Again, this presupposition does not discard the fact that other forms of thought were involved as well. However, the preponderance of the basis to common law, contextual etymology, and terminology within the Declaration and Constitution were clearly Biblical. The well-known statesman Samuel Adams, signer of the Declaration and given the title "the Father of the American Revolution," upon arguing for the rights of colonists would refer to Scripture as the basis of those rights:

> *In the state of nature every man is, under God, judge and sole judge of his own rights... [as Locke writes] 'The natural liberty of man is to be free from any superior power on earth... only to have the Law of nature for his rule'. These may best be understood by reading and carefully studying the institutes of the great Lawgiver and Head of the Christian Church, which are to be clearly written and promulgated in the New Testament.[33]*

There is much more documentation that could be extracted, quoted, and examined concerning the Biblical map and compass at the time of the Declaration and Constitution. Some of this documentation will be elaborated upon later in the main body of this book. However, these citations are but a small sampling and should be sufficient to assure you, the reader, that this author's premise (along with a host of Biblical scholars and heroes much greater than I) of a Biblical map and compass of early America is clearly documented and well founded. History is open to honest investigation, I am simply giving you enough substantiation to be confident and bold to act now.

I particularly challenge men to lead the fight, because a battle it is, and the battle is on. We are not called to a life of ignorance or excess leisure. Instead, "Rise up O men of God, be done with lesser things, give heart and mind and soul and strength unto the King of Kings. Rise up O men of God, the Church for you doth wait!" I would add, your family, your neighbor, your Country for you doth wait to "fight the good fight." Will you?

In case one might want to answer the above question of fighting with an argument toward pacifism, let's explore the Scriptures to find how the question should be answered. There exists a gross caricature of Christians being just about "peace and love."

The Use of Force

The Question of Pacifism: Aren't We Supposed to Just "Love" Everybody?

If we are called to "fight the good fight," which is the Biblical fighting stance, what is the Biblical view of the use of force? What Biblical principles guide us to know when to "turn the other cheek" or when to pull the trigger to stop a deadly threat against you, your family, or your neighbor? Some would argue (quite erroneously, I would say) that we shouldn't even defend ourselves. Actually it is really not that difficult to sort those questions out. Allow me to give to you an overview of the three ways to understand the viewpoints so that you can come to your own Biblical conclusion.

Where the "Rubber meets the Road": Government's and Your Use of Force

A more precise distinction between the Biblical arguments for the use and non-use of force has been clearly explained by theologian Dr. Norman Geisler. Those distinctions are the pacifist, the activist and the selectivist views. The "activist" believes that the Biblical argument for the Christian is all wars ordered by one's government must be fought in obedience to one's government since God ordains government. In complete contrast, the "pacifist" believes the Christian should fight no wars since God has forbidden men to take the lives of others. Finally, the "selectivist" holds that Christians should participate is those wars that are just before God, and indeed not doing so would be disobedience to God.[34] *Each of these views can be applied to your personal ethic of the use (or non-use) of force including your personal defense and the defense of family and neighbor. Once you resolve which is the strongest Biblical argument (and your conviction) you can see how you can extend your view toward a public (as distinct from your personal use of force) when it comes to governmental use of force both within its borders (police) and outside its borders (military).* It is my Biblically-researched and persuaded, personal conclusion that the Biblical ethic calls for the judicious use of force whenever necessary, both on a private level and on a public level of government. This is the "selectivist" position. Due to the limited scope of this book, I will only assume the selectivist view. I will also mention the pacifist position only to point out its errors and inadequacy.

Your Rightful Use of Force

It is plain from Scripture that Jesus taught that the promotion of His eternal Kingdom was not to be done by force. We are not, as God's people, to use force to get people to come to Jesus, to become a Christian. However, let's not pass by the statement that Jesus also clearly made in Luke 22:36. Here, in Holy Scripture, Jesus introduces a clear shift between the Gospel promotion that is not to be by the sword, and then to a distinction of a personal self-defense statement that is to be, "by the sword." He does so with the following striking words, "But now." Please read this passage then pick up again with the following comment. "And He said to them, 'But now, whoever has a money belt is to take it along, likewise also a bag, and whoever has no sword is to sell his coat and buy one'." I won't bore you with the grammatical analysis of this text in the Greek, but I will tell you that Jesus communicated unequivocally to His disciples that, if they didn't own a sword, they must get one even if it means selling one's clothes. Furthermore, the word used for "sword" is an idiom for "war" (Matt. 10:34) or "violent death" (Rom 8:35). Surprised? Yes, Jesus is giving "street-smart" instructions to His Church that they must be armed for self-defense with a deadly weapon! To quote Jesus in a present day manner from the feel of the Greek text, "Men, things are now different, if you don't have a gun, if you've got to sell whatever it takes, get one yesterday!" Theologian Norman Geisler concludes from Jesus' Gospel narratives about swords, "swords are not valid weapons to fight spiritual battles, but they are legitimate tools for one's civil defense. Herein seems to be the sanction of Jesus to the justifiable use of an instrument of death in defense against an unjust aggressor. That is, Jesus commanded the use of the sword as a means of civil defense."[35]

When is the last time you heard this preached from the pulpit? Also consider that Jesus was not without the practice of the use of force against evil when He cleansed the Temple on at least one occasion (Mark 11 and John 2). The "whip" was a weapon of force in His day and His zealous use of it "looks like a clear use of force and the resisting of evildoers."[36] As will be documented later, He may have used this weapon even against people present at the time.

In this chapter of explaining the "building blocks, I don't want to take up space and time to argue the finer points of the "use of force" arguments. Just know that the compelling, Biblical argument is that the use of force by the Christian in opposing evil perpetrators is not simply limited to a couple of passages. A larger, comprehensive Biblical paradigm must be used to base one's conviction on these views rather than mere "verse picking" to prove one's point. The mission of anyone arriving at a theological viewpoint, and the applicable Christian ethic, is to have a comprehensive view of Scripture, "from Genesis to maps," as I call it. These aren't just fancy, theological words being tossed about. What I am trying to communicate to you is that you must have a conviction to the core of your being to know whether you are to pull the trigger and kill someone or not. These are "life and death" decision-building skills! Your view must be in a scientific, textual, and consistent manner so that you are able to decide whether you should take a life or not. So when we finds ourselves placing verses into adversarial positions against each other, we are at fault, not God's revelation. God does not suffer from a multiple personality disorder.

This weakness of "verse picking" is the weakness to the pacifist viewpoint. As Copan and Flannigan stated, "To impose a nonviolent or pacifistic grid on the words and actions of God/Jesus requires significant hermeneutical gymnastics—an approach that creates an interpretive straitjacket."[37] In short, the pacifist position does violence, so to speak, to Biblical interpretation. However, you must be fully convinced before you are placed into having to make a lethal decision.

To shed light on this proper handling of Scripture, I will give you one example of a passage used frequently by the pacifist is Jesus's statement in the Sermon "Whoever slaps you on your right cheek, turn to him the other also" (Matt. 5:39). This statement by our King, when used as a pacifist argument is surgically removed from its historical context. This statement by Jesus is about personal insult, not about physical harm to one's self or others.

Within that cultural context, the striking of the right cheek necessitates a backhanded strike, and "according to Rabbinical Law to hit a man with the back of the hand was twice as insulting as to hit him with the flat of the hand."[38] Alexander Bruce, professor of Apologetics in Glasgow explains, "...the right cheek is only named first according to common custom, (and is) not supposed to be struck first."[39] In other words, Jesus calls one to humbly stand one's ground amid escalating personal insults.

This passage has nothing to do with "use of force" to protect life, it is a prohibition against returning insult for insult. One cannot hold to a nonviolent Jesus or a prohibition of His followers from ever using force without ignoring the overwhelming momentum of the rest of Scripture. Paul, Stephen, John, and the author of Hebrews all preach a God who has, does, and will act with decisive force, "the grid of pacifism/nonviolence seems to go against other affirmations in the New Testament."[40]

The New Testament does not promote a pacifist disposition on God's part nor upon His people. I recently had a delightful conversation with a lady here in Colorado at a Mennonite bakery (the Mennonites are known to be, "pacifists"). This owner/baker confessed to me, "I don't think we Mennonites are really pacifist, we are loving people, but we must fight against evil." This Mennonite woman summed it better than most of us can. The Scriptures indeed teach, "forgiveness and the breaking of evil in society"[41] and to have a "sacrificial, loving response to maintain a non-vindictive, magnanimous, reconciling attitude in all personal relationships when one's own rights or honor are at stake"[42] while at the same time expecting government to do its job of Justice.

An illustration I have used for years to explain this Biblical model is the following: If a Christian man's daughter is raped, he is to expect his government to do its job of Justice while he himself is to choose to forgive the perpetrator and seek to reconcile him to Christ, all the way to the execution chamber. I would add to this illustration in light of this discussion's context the following: the father and his daughter were also obligated to prevent that crime with the use of lethal force against the would-be perpetrator, even if it meant his death, which is an overlying Biblical model as well. The father and/or daughter should have been armed and skillful with a defensive weapon. This illustration now serves to transition into the question of the public ethic, "What is the Biblical role of one's government when it comes to the use of force?"

Your Government's Rightful Use of Force

Without going into too much detail, it is clear from the Scriptures that government does indeed have a God-given right to use force to ensure Righteousness, as only He defines it. The direction God expects government to use force is first within its own borders.

Government's Rightful Use of Force within Its Borders

Later in chapter 2, the case will be carefully laid out that "Romans 13 affirms God does not always carry out divine wrath directly but has partly delegated this task to human governments."[43]

Within this investigation of the use of force, we see God has ordained government's use of force, even deadly force, to administer Justice within its land. The "sword" of Romans 13 is an executioner's sword, "for it is a minister of God, an avenger who brings wrath upon the one who practices evil" (v.4). When we look at the New Testament teachings of Jesus in Matthew 11:21–24, John 2:15, and Mark 11:15–17, we see "Jesus clearly believes in the appropriateness of temporal divine punishment and the Mosaic death penalty."[44] That case for government's legal, God-ordained use of force to maintain Justice and to promote good and peace within the land will later be argued. For now, in explanation of this teacher's writing on the use of force, the simple statement that government has the God-given obligation to enforce Righteousness will stand. The following question of a government's right to wage war against other countries now follows.

Government's Rightful Use of Force against Other Countries

John Calvin made the argument from Scripture, "For if power be given them (government) to preserve tranquility of their dominion... will they allow a whole country to be afflicted and devastated by robberies...to defend by war the dominions entrusted to their safekeeping?"[45] In other words, it is an easy, logical jump from the God-ordained use of force to maintain Justice within its borders to use the same force to defend her citizens from perpetrators outside its borders.

Just as the government's responsibility before God is to promote "good" and restrain "evil" (Romans 13; 1 Peter 2: 13, 14) as God defines them within our borders, so the government must use force against other countries under the same Biblical morals and ethics. *This is where the academic discussion of "just war" begins. There remains a good, Biblical argument for "just war" that can be won, if not by the Biblical weight alone, then by the additional just response to "intolerable aggression" of evil in one's world.*

Albert Einstein was a pacifist. Pastor and theologian Dietrich Bonhoeffer was a pacifist. Croatian theologian Miroslav Volf was a pacifist. That is, until Hitler showed up and unleashed evil upon their land and the world. Einstein would reluctantly argue that the "lesser evil" of the military was necessary to overcome the greater evil of the Third Reich.[46] Recent historical research has shown us that Pastor Bonhoeffer took part in an assassination plan against Hitler and was hung for his selectivist and lethal attempts against the state.[47]

This whole discussion of just war has been argued and discussed since the rise of Constantine by Ambrose of Milan (340–397) and by Augustine (354–430), and into the Reformation with Martin Luther (1483–1546). It continues to be refined today.

Copan and Flannigan set out the seven basic tenets of just war that have been hammered out to this present day:

1. *Just Cause*: All unprovoked aggression is condemned. A war for self-defense and protection (including defense of other vulnerable nations) is morally legitimate. Following this first criterion alone would eliminate all war and aggression.
2. *Just Intent*: The only legitimate intention is to secure a just or fair peace for friend and foe alike, ruling out revenge, conquest, economic gain, or ideological supremacy. Ultimately, greater good than harm should result from war. "Vengeance, subjugation, and conquest are unjustifiable purposes." Sometimes there are "unintentional effects" (killing civilians) which accompany the intended effect of restraining violence.

3. *Lawful Declaration*: Only a lawful government has the right
    to initiate war. Only a state—not individuals or parties
    within the state—can legitimately exercise this authority.[48]

These three Biblical criteria are crucial in understanding that
the very terms and definitions behind the terms used, "just," "lawful," and "morally legitimate" are founded upon a Biblical derivation
and application from centuries of argument and discussion from
godly men and women within the Church. These three criteria, I
believe, rightly define the selectivist defense of the use of force arguments when it comes to God-ordained, governmental responsibilities
to God, her citizens, and against evil intrusion by other countries or
political entities. A provocative question can now be asked based on
current events. Based on the government's responsibility toward us
as citizens, is not the erection of a protective border wall part of the
government's duty toward us? I will let you decide.

With these building blocks having now been laid out for your
serious consideration, we will proceed into the body of this book. We
can now unfold the Biblical, historical, and legal argument to this
timeless truth, stated as my theme for this book: "God's people and
her respective governments have both responsibilities and boundaries
toward one another, mutual force guaranteeing that balance." Let's
continue now to look at the heart of God and what He has to say
about these "fighting words."

We will now move from the word picture of "building blocks"
to the fighting analogy of "lines in the sand" that are drawn that
invite use of force, if crossed.

CHAPTER 2

꧁❦꧂

Government's Lines in the Sand: Their Responsibilities

Introductory Shocker: The Church Has a Delegated Authority over Government

What? How dare one propose that the Church has any authority over government? After all, we have a sacred "separation of Church and state"! Let me push you a bit further then. The Church not only has a delegated authority over the state here in the United States, this is true for each and every government in the world.

Listen carefully as there are fine lines of distinction to draw here. Within the previous chapter, we investigated the first building block, that there is an aspect to how God's people are to be redemptive on a societal level to bring the "Kingdom of God" into our culture and society. Our understanding of "Righteousness" and "Justice" are to come from God and into the world (our culture and government). "Salvation," even in the "here and now" sense, is to permeate the world around us. God's intent and plan is to do this through you!

All societies, all governments around the world are under the authority of Christ and His Kingdom, regardless of whether they acknowledge it or not. You, the reader, and we, the Church, are the God-ordained Kingdom agents of conscience for government. Historically we have proven that to be true over and over again.

Throughout time, God's people have shaped history and nations for the better; we are a force to be reckoned with!

Do you have your seat belts on? I'm about to send you crashing into a lie you may have bought into. The First Amendment was stated in such a way as to prohibit government from interfering with the Church, but not the other way around! (Please read it for yourself!)

Before delving into government's boundaries and responsibilities of authority before God, the context must be set by asking the question why and how it is that God's Kingdom is to be applied on a societal level and therefore in government? *Although we are not dealing with the "study of sin" directly at this point, theologian Millard Erickson brings up an often neglected aspect to the social dimension of sin which will lead to my next discussion of how God's redemptive work is to be applied to the social dimension and government as well. He points out that "Scripture also makes frequent reference to group or collective sin" and that God speaks to "oppressive conditions for which He holds society responsible," and that we, as a corporate society, "contribute to these evils through financial involvement (by paying taxes or dues), direct approval (by voting), or tacit consent (by not disagreeing or registering opposition)." [1]*

As the Body of Christ, His Church, we revel in God's grace applied to us in our eternal salvation. However, this societal dimension of God's redemption is mostly neglected, leading to the demise of our culture and our obedience to our King. I state this axiom frequently: It is not a question of what has happened to our culture; our cultural deterioration is a statement that the Church has not happened!

The first step is to admit to the obvious: that sin has affected the entire world, and that, just as we have individually sinned, we also corporately sinned from a community to a national and global level. In other words, sin dysfunction extends not just to every aspect of each individual's being but also to the universality of all human beings and their collectives, both society and governments.

Equally true is in like manner that the redemption and grace of God that has affected the individual and the Church eternally, are also meant to influence all of culture around us in this temporal, "here and now" manner. The "Kingdom of God," however imperfectly visible this side of heaven, is to be a transformational force for God's glory in the midst of this broken world. As we will discover in a later chapter, it will be shown that this transformational force of God's Kingdom is to applied to man's Kingdom, or government, and our culture as well.

Now, let's explore this often-misunderstood reality of the "Kingdom of God." Concerning the manifestation of God's Kingdom in this temporal world, this I have already noted in the previous chapter that too much can be made of fine distinctions about what is meant by the "Kingdom of God," this book is not meant to be a seminary lesson on such. Christ's entrance into our world was announced by John the Baptist in Matthew 3:2 with the phrase "The Kingdom of God is at hand." Again, I will not bore you with all the grammatical analysis. If you want that, you can read my doctoral dissertation. Just know that this text is a declaration that the Kingdom of God is, first, from heaven itself, and second, the Kingdom of God is now here and is meant to stay. Alexander Bruce, professor of Apologetics in Glasgow, called this a "legal announcement" upon earth.[2]

In concert with the Baptist's announcement, Jesus Himself teaches us to pray, "Thy Kingdom come, Thy will be done, on earth as it is in heaven" (Matt. 6:10). *The grammar here uses two imperatives ("come," and "be done"), depicting immediacy and cooperative responsibility to the plea.* Clearly inherent within that prayer is a sense of personal responsibility as citizens of God's Kingdom in full cooperation with that which is now brought into effect, up close and personal to this world, through Christ's inaugural ministry.

The Book of Acts closes with the summation of the Apostle Paul's ministry in his closing years as him "preaching the Kingdom of God and teaching concerning the Lord Jesus Christ" (Acts 28:31). The Body of Christ in her very essence is a citizenry of Christ's Kingdom. "Although the Church is not the Kingdom of God…the Church is the instrument of the Kingdom of God…and the Church is the custodian of the Kingdom of God."[3].

Most Christians miss the Biblical teaching on God's Kingdom, which has now arrived in "seed form" with Christ's ministry and is yet still to come in full fruition. Charles Colson states this same frustrated misunderstanding was what caused the Jews to be confused in Christ's day: "Another reason that the Jews missed the full significance of the message of the Kingdom of God was that Jesus spoke about a Kingdom that had come and a Kingdom that was yet to come—one Kingdom in two stages. This still confuses people today."[4]

"Salvation" impacts the Chosen Body of Christ, but there is also to be, in God's plan, a temporal yet contagious redemption of society and nations as the Kingdom of God. Christ has announced His all-pervading Lordship: "All authority is given to me in heaven and on earth" (Matt. 28:18) in His preamble to the Great Commission. It is to you, the reader, and it is your calling to announce that reminder of His Lordship over all humankind! All rulers and all governments, regardless of geography, nationality, or form of government, are under His rule, whether they acknowledge or even recognize it right now. His work in us despite our imperfections is to be a seasoning for the earth: "You are the salt of the earth" (Matt.5:13).

Our liberty in Christ is meant for us to be lights of His Justice: "You are the light of the world...Let your light shine before men in such a way as they may see your good works, and glorify your Father who is in heaven" (Matt. 5:14, 16). This sense of the triumphant Church heralding God's Kingdom drove God's people to build a nation (the United States in particular), produce universities (Harvard and Yale, for example), abolish slavery (at least in England and the United States), and to build more orphanages and hospitals than any other nation in world history!

This work of God does not mean we are to bring about a utopia here on earth *(a postmillennial view of history);* it simply recognizes the Church as more than a narcissistic, self-absorbed, and apathetic Body only concerned with itself. We are called to be history makers! We are called to be culture transformers! We are called by God to resist and oppose evil as agents of His Kingdom. We are the people of God and therefore a force to be reckoned with, bent as an ordained institution on the offense in the world to glorify God in every dimension upon earth, whether it is the legal system, the arts, education, the helping of the poor, and, as it applies here, your government and society.

Church, people with a moral compass, yes, you, the reader, are to draw the line in the sand for government! On the one hand within the eternal command of God, we are to seek to persuade men to Christ and to introduce them to His eternal salvation. Then on the other hand, within the cultural command from God, we are to introduce Christ the King to all of humankind and to persuade them that His Truth, His Law brings wholeness and redemption to people and society. This is not an either-or work of God through us; rather, it is a both-and mandate from God.

Many of us have only heard one side of the story, the one that focuses on people's eternal standing with God. The other orders from our King have been largely ignored and neglected. It does no good to separate these two, the salvation of men and the redemption of culture, into two camps, as God Himself does not. To do so would be just as erroneous as to separate "make disciples of all men" (Matt. 25:19) from "Let you light shine before all men" (Matt.5:16). Just as the Body of Christ is not to expect complete fulfillment or perfection of the eternal mandate to "make disciples," for example, neither is she to expect the same perfect fulfillment with the cultural mandate. Again, we are not here to bring about social or governmental perfection.

You are here, by God's sovereign Hand, in your time, in your place to pray and to act upon: "Thy Kingdom come, Thy will be done."! These twin mandates are from our King to us, His people. We are to, as the old hymn states, "Work till Jesus comes." You are on a winning battleship; get involved and fight with the winning team!

The responsibilities and boundaries of God's people in relationship to government will be investigated in later chapters following this one. For now, we will begin by looking into the responsibilities and boundaries of government in light of God's Kingdom in your present history.

Government: Imperfection Is to Be Expected

Here is a "no brainer" statement that we often overlook: there is no perfect government because there is no such thing as a perfect person or persons. Perhaps it seems trivial to discuss what is inherently obvious within Scriptures and in your experience, "for all have sinned and fall short of the glory of God." (Rom. 3:23) The infection of sin into this world—or "evil," as it will be used here—extends to both individuals and to any collection of individuals, including government.

Luke 4:5–6 is an interesting insight into how Satan sees governing authorities: "I will give you all this domain and its glory; for it has been handed over to me, and I give it to whomever I wish." Satan is partially correct, except for his denial of God's sovereignty over him and over men in authority. As Chafer points out about this passage, "…it is clearly indicated that the governments of this world system are under Satan's authority. So, also in John 5:27 and in 1Corinthians 15:27 it is revealed that all authority has been committed to Christ by the Father. Eventually Christ will put down all finite rule and authority (1 Cor. 15:25, 28)."[5] For now in this time, there is this tension between Christ's Kingdom and Satan's Kingdom, and humanity is the stage upon which God's sovereign Hand is guiding. However, the Biblical truth is that He has called us into that tension, that battle.

Please understand that we do not wish to diminish nor minimalize the good of individuals and to any collection of individuals who display "good" reflecting the "image of God" stamped in us since Creation. Many, many "good" things, even in God's eyes, occur all over this globe through people. That is because of the "image of God" is infused into every human being's invisible DNA. The focus of this book is on the Biblical reality of sin and God's perspective of human government.

Within that focus, as we will see, it is God's will that human government exist. Government of men is not meant to be, and has never meant to be a solution for evil in the world. It is not, nor ever has been, a vehicle propelling the hope of a human utopia. God did not give us government to solve all of our problems! (Did I just hear a chorus of "Duh!" just now?) Our current belief system in America in which government is here to take care of us is inherently false and in opposition to God. Government is made up of, in differing forms, fallen human beings. "Civil government does not set the boundaries of human behavior. The state is not a remedy for sin, but a means to restrain it."[6]

That is what we are to fight for. Not a utopian government but a government simply operating, however imperfectly, to restrain evil within our society without apology. Given that Biblical reality and the reality of Christ's reign as King of the universe, we will turn to investigate why God thought it necessary to have human government.

"The Necessary Evil" of Government

Bonhoeffer succinctly cites the Biblical view and source of human government: "Government is divinely ordained authority to exercise worldly dominion by divine right. Government is deputyship for God on earth. It can be understood only from above. Government does not proceed from society, but it orders society from above."[7] Colson humorously stated, "The origin of government goes back to humanity's first sin, when to keep rebellious Adam and Eve away from the Tree of Life, God stationed an angel with a flaming sword at the entrance of the Garden; this was, so to speak, the first cop on the beat."[8]

Jesus and Pilate once had a political discussion. Jesus makes it very clear to Pilate where his governmental authority came from. When frustrated with Jesus's unintimidated disposition toward him, Pilate resorts to vaunting his governmental authority at Jesus to remind Him he could have Him alternately set free or crucified. Jesus simply states the legal fact from the Law of God, "You would not have even begun to have this authority over me at all if it already had not been given to you from above" (John 19:10–11, my translation from the Greek text).

Jesus's authoritative declaration over Pilate evidently frightened him enough so that immediately following these words from Jesus, "Pilate kept trying to release Him" (v. 12, my translation from the Greek text). An important interpretive observation must be made here: Jesus states that Pilate's (and by extension, Rome's) authority was established by heaven. It can be easily derived that it was God who gave the authority to sinful Pilate and sinful Rome in her governmental authority; it is God's will that government be in place, however imperfect it is. Therefore, we have an "evil" system that is "necessary"—that is, a "necessary evil." This principle does not expound on how well Pilate and Rome were exercising their authority delegated by God, only the reality from God's point of view that it was so. The lesson from Jesus in this political discussion is clear: God's people, throughout time, must view their own governments as God's institution and under God's authority.

The conclusion from Scripture seems clear enough. First, human government is not perfect. It will always consist of fallen human beings. Second, despite fallen humanity, God has instituted, or established, human government. Third, because human government is a fallen but necessary institution, the authority comes from not within government but from without and above, God Himself. Government is a "necessary evil" designed by God for the order of society.

Here is the critical clincher you must hang on to: since God has instituted human, governmental authority, it is not a Law unto itself; God has a hand in the government's responsibilities to its citizens and boundaries to its authority based upon His Law and His character. Francis Schaeffer concludes, "God has ordained the State as a *delegated* authority; it is not autonomous."[9] Since then, God ordains government, yet at the same time it is under His Kingship; we can see now why human government has been termed a "necessary evil."

The next question must now be asked: "Where are some" lines in the sand" of responsibility and boundaries that God has placed upon this 'necessary evil'?"

Line in the Sand 1 for Government Responsibility: Christ Is King over Government

Although the Biblical principles as it pertains to God and government are applicable to all human governments, the focus here and its application takes place within the United States of America. Therefore, the direct applications will apply to the Constitution of the United States and, where applicable, her Declaration of Independence.

Behind both the United States government's Constitution and the inseparable document of the Colonies' Declaration of Independence are an undergirding Biblical map and a Biblical compass that overshadows the key ideas and language of these documents. The Founders clearly understood the above "clincher" that God instituted government so it is not a Law to itself. They understood that government was not to have a free reign upon people. In fact, they broke from a nation (England) whose monarch (King George) had started doing just that.

An example of this Biblical map is a quote from James Madison Jr., who was a political theorist, American statesman, and served as the fourth president of the United States: "Before any man can be considered as a member of Civil Society, he must be considered as a subject of the Governor of the Universe."[10]

One of the key phrases within the Declaration is "Nature and Nature's God," reflecting both Enlightenment thinking and the Great Awakening theology of Jonathan Edwards. This phrase is within the Declaration's preamble and gives the rational basis for the Colonies' dissolution of the political bands of King George. *Although its phraseology comes from a variety of sources, it is principally recognition of God as He has revealed Himself in General Revelation. Cursory readings from the American founders' writings amply demonstrate that the cultural milieu within the Colonies was a Biblical consensus; terminology that was used in the United States's Declaration and Constitution were within the* sitz im leben *(setting in life) of a Judeo-Christian ethic. Charles Colson states, "Religion (in the Judeo-Christian sense) has always been a decisive factor in the shaping of the American experience."[11]*

British observer G. K. Chesterton stated the fabric of America succinctly as "a nation with the soul of a Church"[12] All this simply branches from the statement by Jesus Christ that Pilate's, Rome's and, ultimately, all government's authority "had been given you from above" (John 19:11, my translation).

Line in the Sand 2:
Government has Responsibilities to You under God

You are about to get your eyes opened! The entire purpose of the following statements are to give you a Biblical platform for what the Church, the Bride of Christ, is to expect from her government, at any time in history and in any geographical location.

As we delve into these truths that may well revolutionize your life and that of others, please remember that this book is not intended to be either a legal brief or a legal argument. Why? Because I am afraid of the law? No; rather, Law is in second place: that would be arguing from a lesser authority (law) to a larger one (Biblical theology). In other words, theology (God's mind, heart, and will revealed) informs law, not the other way around. We understand the nature and parameters of Law through God's revelation.

Therefore, we will now investigate responsibilities of your government from the highest authority platform of God's word, God's "Law," to the lesser authority platforms of humankind. The following will give the Biblical platform for you and for the people of God to speak to her government in an authoritative manner as citizens of God's Kingdom. You will be incited to be the prophetic voice from the King of the universe to her human governmental kings. This is your calling! This is your personalized mission from your King who gave His life for you.

First Responsibility: Government Has an Obligation to Submit to the Constitution

There is a legal, moral, and ethical obligation of the United States government's responsibility to be in a submissive posture to the Constitution. That may sound like a mere cliché, but God Almighty thinks otherwise. As citizens of God's Kingdom, we are to expect our governments to have a righteous fidelity to their legally binding contracts and constitutions.

Let's look at a clear confession from our own government: A US Congress publication entitled "Our American Government" begins with an opening question, "What is the purpose of the US Government?" The response is decidedly clear:

> The purpose is expressed in the preamble to the Constitution: 'We the people of the United States, in Order to form a more perfect union, establish Justice, insure domestic Tranquility, provide for the common defense, *promote the general Welfare, and secure the Blessings of Liberty to ourselves and our Prosperity, do ordain and establish this Constitution for the United States of America.* [13]

This quotation from the Constitution's preamble quoted by our own government is replete with terminology that recognizes the Biblical ethics of the writers of the Constitution: *Justice, welfare, blessings,* and even *liberty* and *prosperity.* A following question then asks, "What is the Constitution?" Their answer is, "The Constitution is the basic and supreme Law of the United States. It prescribes the structure of the U.S. Government, provides the legal foundation on which all its actions must rest, and enumerates and guarantees the rights due to all its citizens."[14] In short, the Constitution, and its inseparable document, the Declaration of Independence, are legally and morally binding documents both among the citizens of the United States and between the citizens of the United States and her government.

Get this straight! These documents delegate authority to the government and not the other way around. By its own admission and declaration our Congress states the legal, ethical and moral obligation for the US government to stand under, and not above, nor even beside, the Constitutional Contract. To do otherwise is a legal and moral breach of contract by the government.

The King over governments does not take contractual breaches lightly. There is judgment by God for contractual breach: *"It is better that you should not vow than that you should vow and not pay"*

(Ecclesiastes 5:5). *"I tell you that every careless word [broken prom-ise] that people speak, they shall give an accounting for it in the Day of Judgment"* (Matthew 12:36). To breach the Covenantal Contract of the US Constitution is to step out of the delegated authority assigned by the Constitution. Furthermore, directly implicit to the Constitutional Contract's parties involved is a third party witnessing to this document found in the phrase "Nature's God." The bottom line: breaking contract with the Constitution is to breach God's trust.

Here is a contemporary example. President Trump sought out his second appointment to the Supreme Court of the United States. This nomination by Trump, Brett Kavanaugh, finally cleared the Senate floor but only with a malicious and false defamation attempt against him. The war was red-hot because Kavanaugh, as does any Conservative judge, sees the Constitution and its authority for what it is in its original meaning, and the author's original intent (strict construction-ism). "Progressives" have sought to go around this very authority of the Constitution we speak of here by redefining the essence of the Constitution as an evolving, "living and breathing" document. This view is an attempt to emasculate the Constitution's authority over government. In short, the choice and the ensuing cultural and governmental war presently going on is between:

1. Return to the original meaning of the US Constitution, by which the Founding Fathers so wisely established limited government and individual rights (the Constructionism view). Rights are derived from God and not government in this option.

2. Continue down the path of judicial activism by means of stripping the Constitution of its authority (making government the ultimate authority and power) through redefinition and recreation (the living-document view), and watch our government and our individual rights deteriorate right before our eyes. The anchor of defining morality is cut from our Country's ship, rights are lost under this option, and the power of the government continually increases in arrogance against God.

This is precisely why liberal activists and those of our liberal culture will fight the appointment of any Constructionism judge like Kavanaugh. The Constitution, as it was written, is deemed a threat of authority over the government. Remember the statement "It prescribes the structure of the U.S. Government, provides the legal foundation on which all its actions must rest, and enumerates and guarantees the rights due to all its citizens" quoted a page earlier? The US Constitution is a God-honoring contract between government and its citizens, with God as a witness. If you understand this basic overview of what our Constitution is, what it represents, and why our government must submit to it, you will understand why this war in our government and culture exists and why we, the people of God, must fight this evil.

The liberal activists realize this was not about Kavanaugh; it was about the God-honoring Constitution of authority over them! Since you now understand this, you too will be hated by them because you have now drawn a line in the sand threatening their power! To use the common colloquialism, "Them's fightn' words!"

Second Responsibility: Government Has an Obligation of Submission to "Nature and Nature's God"

Still a deeper line in the sand than the previous truth is what the following. This phrase "Nature and Nature's God" within our founding Documents is critical because it defines the Biblical statement of who government is derived from. *"The mission of government to serve Christ is at the same time its inescapable destiny…no matter whether it is conscious or unconscious to this mission or even whether it is true or untrue to it," declared theologian Dietrich Bonhoeffer.*[15] Government is not only bound to the Constitution that delegates its authority, but more importantly, government is bound to God who has created its institution and delegated its authority (and, by default, the Constitution's authority).

I would echo Bonhoeffer's Biblical conviction: the prophetic rubric for the citizens of God's Kingdom is to declare the Lordship of Christ to all governing authorities. As God's people, it is our moral obligation to stand up to and speak to government about its moral responsibilities and boundaries before God.

Third Responsibility: Government Must Punish Evil with Delegated Authority from God

Governments "are established by God" to "give praise" for "good behavior" and to "bring wrath on the one who practices evil" (Rom. 13:1–4). These verses describe government's God-delegated responsibility to punish or execute people for evil deeds. The "Rule of Law" is defined by "Nature's God" and applied judiciously and equally to all without exception; President or peasant, wealthy or impoverished, black, white, brown, or green.

We have already established that God, and not the state, defines the moral phrases in these verses. As "ministers ("deacons" in the Greek text) of God" (v. 4), Copan and Flannigan remark that, "Romans 13 affirms that God does not always carry out divine wrath directly but has partly delegated this task to human governments."[16] It is therefore of great moral necessity that a government recognizes her role before God and defines moral behavior as He does, and not as they might. They are to bear "God's wrath" upon evil as delegated by Him, and not their own devised wrath derived from their own derived "law."

These verses in Romans 13 instruct us that the government is in a trust to honor Him and to govern her citizens as under God. *Perhaps the perception of this understanding was clearly elucidated by the present British Monarch, Queen Elizabeth II, when she entitled her recent book* The Servant Queen and the King She Serves. *Within that title the Queen sees herself as under King Jesus and in a servant hood position with her subjects, thus defining her monarchy. She rightly understands that as a governmental monarch she is in a trust with God to serve her subjects, to love God and men in the spirit of "the Great Commandment."*

This godly, submissive disposition by Queen Elizabeth II runs contrary to most governments. "Government by nature seeks power and will always attempt to generate its own moral legitimacy for its decisions. Inevitably, it resents any group that attempts to act as its conscience."[17] It is because of this clear contrast between the Queen's posture before the King and past US President Barack Obama's posture before the King that I had concluded I would rather live under a monarchial government that recognizes King Jesus than in a democratic republic that has now dismissed Him from their courts. However, I for one will fight to bring our Democratic Republic back under their legally and morally submissive posture before God.

Fourth Responsibility: Government Must Love God and People

Sounds kind of strange, does it not? Government is to "love" God and people? Let's get a context. "Love of God and love of man are involved also in the responsibilities to the state…in official social relations a principle of Justice prevails…"[18]

A famous American theologian, Carl F. H. Henry, here indicates that the Great Commandment is a rule of Law imposed on the state to enact Justice. One of the primary responsibilities of government is to love its citizens by understanding and protecting their God given "rights." What is at stake, as Colson states, "is the use of power, whether for personal gain or for the state's ordained function, which is at issue."[19] The issue is that the state is to "love God and to love men" by protecting their God-given rights. This is absolutely critical for us to understand! The government only recognizes our God-given rights; they do not grant them to us! I repeat, government does not give or grant us rights, they can only recognize our God-given rights and protect them for us; that's "love" from government!

Let me give you a personal example. As a weapons instructor, I often "open carry" my handgun here in Colorado (this method opens up a lot of great conversations). People remark, "Oh, I see you are a big Second Amendment supporter." My reply stuns them, "No, I carry a handgun as a duty and right before God to protect myself and others. Our Second Amendment only happens to recognize that God-given right!" The Second Amendment is a government recognition, not a grantor, of that right. My US government is loving you and I by recognizing that right to protect ourselves against evil. Furthermore, more to the Second Amendment's purpose, our US

government is loving us protect ourselves should she become tyrannical (more on this later).

Fifth Responsibility: The Protection of Citizen's "Rights"

You will see an overlap between the previous governmental
responsibility to love God and people and this fifth responsibility
they have. The US Congressional publication documented earlier
used the phrase, "rights due to all citizens." It is not in a vacuum of
ideas from which they pulled this idea.

*Samuel Adams was an American statesman, political philosopher,
and one of the Founding Fathers of the United States. In a publication
addressing the "Rights of Colonists," he states, "Among the Natural rights
of the colonists are these: first, a right to life; second, to liberty; third, to
property; together to support and defend them in the best manner they
can. These are...commonly called the first Law of nature." Lest one presupposes merely Enlightenment or semideistic ideals within Adam's writing here, he further elucidates, "These (rights) may be best understood by
reading and carefully studying the institutes of the great Lawgiver and
Head of the Christian Church, which are to be found clearly written and
promulgated in the New Testament."* [20]

It is indeed true that there is a delicate blend of Christian theology and Enlightenment thinking in this understanding of "rights,"
but that does not annul the Biblical theology behind government's
protection of "rights" as a Biblical mandate to government. John
Whitehead is recognized as one of America's top constitutional attor-
neys specializing in religious freedom. Upon this point, he explains,

> Human beings are destined by nature, if not by,
> "Nature's God" for certain ends and therefore
> are endowed with certain rights, which must be
> acknowledged and respected by law. This tradi-
> tional approach to rights was recognized by the
> deistically inclined among the founding fathers

and was compatible with the Christian view that
rights are the specific endowment of the personal
Creator God of the Bible.[21]

Sixth Responsibility: Government Must Recognize the Lawgiver to Administer Our Laws

Another means of government loving God and men is to properly apply its delegated authority by rightfully administrating "Law." *Although later we will delve into the question of "What is law?" a quick overview is in order. When Jesus was in discussion with Pilate, He made a declarative statement about His Kingdom and His rule of Law, "My Kingdom is not of this world" (John 18:36). From a syntactical point of view, Jesus states that His Kingdom "is not sourced out of this world" (i.e., He is transcendent over and above this world). He will later declare Pilate's authority as delegated from Him, or "from above" (John 19:11)—that is, from God above, not men below.*

Constitutional authorities recognize this relationship between transcendent Law and our government. "Law in the true sense is bibliocentric, concerned with Justice in terms of the Creator's revelation."[22] When it comes to the cultural map and compass of the Declaration and the US Constitution, Joseph Story, professor of Law at Harvard University said, "The Constitution was acknowledging that a system of absolutes exists upon which government and Law can be founded."[23]

The simple point is this: God's "Law" rules over and is to define man's "law." It is only within the context of God's transcendent (above and beyond) Law which is only delegated to a government so that it can administer "law" faithfully and submissively before Him. In this proper use of its authority, government is fulfilling her calling to "love God and people." God loves His creation, and He loves to see His creation flourish with His creative order. God's Law, from which we are to derive our "laws," is meant to bless and nurture people in healthy, prosperous living in our culture.

Seventh Responsibility: Government Is Obligated to Preserve God's Definition of Morality

One of the critical roles of government before God is the preservation of a civil, moral society. *"The Founders thought the government had a role in promoting good character among the citizen body, because the liberty which it is government's job to protect is inseparable from virtue. Moral education or character formation, which begins with the family, is necessary for the preservation of a free society."* [24] Charles Colson reminds us that "when God established ancient Israel as a nation; His first order of business was the propagation of law, not just for religious purposes, but for the ordering of civil life."[25] Bottom line? Government does not invent morality. It is to preserve the King of king's definition of morality.

It is indeed God's will that government be in place to be "a minister of God to you for good" and who "brings wrath on the one who practices evil" (Rom. 13:3–4). Please note the following carefully because there is so much confusion in this area: There is the government's godly role as a morality guard that is to be clearly distinct from your personal ethic of grace and forgiveness. The Christian citizen's public ethical expectation from government is that they uphold a standard distinct from their own personal disposition.

"The state has a different role in God's economy. Its business is not to forgive rapists and murderers but rather to punish evildoers."[26] It is the state's God-given responsibility to maintain morality within her country using proper punishment, even the death penalty if called for. *"Paul picks up on the 'revenge' and 'wrath of God' in 12:19, stating that the state is the 'avenger of evil' to bring 'wrath' on evildoers"*[27] According to Romans 13, not only is government to punish evil that has been already committed, but they have a responsibility to preserve society from evil. *In fact, "Biblical scholar N. T. Wright takes the view that force—yes, even lethal force-may be necessary to stop criminals from doing their worst."*[28] You, as a disciple of Christ must seek to forgive the mass shooter who killed your spouse while expecting your government to execute the killer. Those are not inconsistent. Both are consistently right with God. You the citizen must act proactively in both of these areas before God!

The early founders of the United States undoubtedly saw the benefits of a moral society and the necessity of religious ethics among her citizens. Noting the Biblical history of the Jews, John Adams stated, "If I were an atheist...I should believe that chance had ordered the Jews to preserve and propagate to all mankind the doctrine of a supreme, intelligent, wise, almighty sovereign of the universe, which I believe to be the great essential principle of all morality, and consequently, of all civilization."[29]

Adam's famous statement sums up the ethical map of our Country's foundations: "Our constitution was made only for a moral and religious people, it is wholly inadequate for the government of any other," with George Washington echoing the same perspective: "Of all the dispositions and habits which lead to political prosperity religion and morality are indispensable supports."[30]

A strong moral base was inherently sought, encouraged, and protected by America's earliest founders. The Biblical ethical codes were that which were prominent *so that Solzhenitsyn would observe, "rights were granted on the ground that man is God's creature. That is, freedom was given to the individual conditionally, in the assumption of his constant religious responsibility."[31]*

The whole phrase coined by Thomas Jefferson, "separation of Church and state," has been clearly and grossly misrepresented today. Although John Adams, our second president to the United States, shared in religious liberal views to that of Thomas Jefferson, his "commitment to state support for organized religion was due to the Church's positive moral influence upon society." [32] Adams fought for financial state support of the Massachusetts's Church because of the moral good the Church brought, clearly a different perspective on the First Amendment than that which is propounded today. The "separation of Church and state" is an absolute lie used for deceptive control, and is not to be found in the First Amendment!

The conclusion from Biblical theology and the early American founder's comments is that it is the responsibility of government before God to preserve and enforce moral virtue in her society. That "moral virtue" is clearly dictated by God's standards and is reflected by the Biblical consensus of the day. The focus of those specific areas which require a moral guard is many, but we can briefly review them now.

Government Must Preserve Our Country's Morality

The government's responsibility for moral preservation begins with internal or "intranational" order. There is also the arena of the government protecting its citizens from external threats, which will be addressed next. For now, we will look at three general areas of importance.

Government Must Protect the God-Given Rights of Life, Liberty, and Property

William Blackstone was an eighteenth-century jurist whose publication "Commentaries on the Law of England" set the standard for England, the early Colonies, and later the United States as a Judeo-Christian base for jurisdictional law. Whitehead sums up Blackstone's Biblical basis of property ownership in early America:

> Blackstone argued that the cultural mandate given to Adam and Eve in Genesis 1 is the basis for man's possession of property. This divine mandate was the only true basis for the right to hold private property or, for that matter, any right. In Blackstone's view, and in the eyes of those who founded the United States, every right or Law comes from God, and the very words, *rights, laws, freedoms* and so on are meaningless without their divine origin.[33]

Rev. Prof. Samuel Rutherford was a Scottish Presbyterian pastor, theologian, and author whose formidable work *Lex Rex* became the cornerstone of thinking through the Biblical ethics of government and man's relationship to it. He wrote, "The natural liberty of man is to be free from any superior power on earth, and not to be under the will or legislative authority of man, but only to have the Law of nature for his rule."[34] What do you think about that? Are you, are we, there now?

When Samuel Adams reflected upon Rutherford's statement, Samuel Adams wrote, "Among the natural rights of the colonists are these: first, a right to life; second, to liberty; third, to property."[35] These three, known as "Locke's Triad"—life, liberty, and property—became the foundation of basic rights of humanity before God that government were to protect. It was such a foundation for moral preservation that when it was originally written into the Declaration of Independence, the word *property* had to be reworded by Jefferson as "the pursuit of happiness" so as to not confuse slaves as property in the issue.[36]

Government Must Protect the God-Given Institution of Marriage

Genesis 1 clearly indicates God's priority in creating marriage. Despite the popular rumor (and humor), neither labor nor marriage is the result of the Curse from The Fall, but were rather created and blessed before sin entered the world.

Marriage is a "Creation right" of mankind before God; the State neither creates nor gives the right to marriage. The state cannot create, nor can the state establish marriage, as it belongs to God since the Garden even before the Fall.[37] For this reason, whenever I would perform marriage ceremonies, I would state that, as a minister, I was acting only as a "witness" for the state, and not acting by the state's authority, despite the traditional verbiage of, "by the authority of the State of..."

The responsibility of government, therefore, is to only acknowledge and rightly regulate marriage as before God's law. The current trend of the state that is both immoral and treacherous before God and against humanity in falsely creating so-called marriage between same-sex or sexually mutated people can be seen as nothing but the state stepping out of its proper role of authority. Such action by the state immediately makes those actions null and void by God.

God's people, therefore, cannot honor the state's illicit actions as law, nor comply with them. Government's responsibility concerning marriage are under the authority of God's Law for marriage, and must be regulated among its citizens as such. Any other actions or laws from the state are to be considered void and illegal before God. Governmental laws and actions honoring God's Law of marriage are to be respected and honored.

Government Must Protect God's Gift of Labor

As stated earlier, labor was created by God in the Garden. "Be fruitful and multiply, and fill the earth, and subdue it; and rule over the fish of the sea and over the birds of the sky and over every living thing that moves on the earth…I have given you every plant…and every tree yielding seed; it shall be food for you" (Gen. 1:28–29). One cannot be sure how much or what kind of labor was involved, but it was apparently given as a blessing from God from the outset. Only later would the Curse taint but not obliterate labor as a blessing from God (3:17–19).

> *He was to govern nature in order to develop to the full its potential for reflecting the glory of God and promote the well-being of man. Nature bore by creation and preservation the impress of the Divine Mind. Man is not to work independently of God. This broad command that man is to subdue the earth gives legitimate standing to the enterprise of science.*[38]

It is an individual's responsibility to labor and provide for his own basic needs. The Apostle Paul lays out the Christian work ethic or the Biblical model for labor: "we did not eat anyone's bread without paying for it, but with labor and hardship we kept working night and day so that we would not be a burden on any of you" (2 Thess. 3:8). Government and "society do not owe the poor a living; it owes them a way to make a living."[39] Rather, "if anyone is not willing to work, then he is not to eat either" (2 Thess. 3:10). It is a sick overreach for government to enable laziness, or an "entitlement" mentality for those who are able to work. It is to strip humans of their *image dei* (image of God) to reflect God's creative labor when an able-bodied person is enabled not to labor. This Biblical principle being addressed here applies to the able-bodied only, and is not directly applicable to those who are not able to work.

The focus of this chapter is only to teach you that it is the government's responsibility to encourage productive labor, and to ensure that commerce, culture, science, and art are reflective of God's attributes. As far as government is concerned, we see three Biblical responsibilities: First, labor is a blessing from God, not a gift from government; it is a right from God, not from government. Second, as a right and blessing from God, government's responsibility is to encourage labor and industry among her citizens. It is not to enable irresponsible laziness in those who are able to work. Third, the responsibility of government is to regulate labor only in its ethics of Justice and Righteousness as defined by God. Labor that does not reflect the nature of God or the good of society is to be discouraged and halted by government. We, the citizens, we, the Church, are to hold government's "feet to the fire" on the eternal principles.

So not only is government under God to preserve morality within our Country, it is also to protect us from evil desiring to invade our borders.

Government Is to Morally Protect Us from International Threats

We have already looked into "pacifism versus activism" and "just war," and it has already been addressed in chapter 1. However, let's quickly relook at the Biblical data here so as to establish the governmental responsibility of moral preservation.

One can simply conclude what is said in Romans 13 about "state officials whose role has been ordained of God to *protect* the innocent, to *preserve* the peace (c.f. 1 Tim. 2:1–2), and to *punish* evildoers"[40] and apply it to the wider obligation of doing the same internationally to protect its citizenry. Croatian theologian and Yale professor Miroslav Volf, once a pacifist and critic of the use of force, now states, "I do think that a military response may be appropriate in cases of intolerable aggression. I find that I am not that far from a just-war theory as I thought I was." [41]

The notable theologian Carl F. H. Henry, from his observations of the Biblical data and its application toward Christian ethics, summarized his observations by saying, "A nation which runs its affairs…committed to nonresistance of aggressions against it—is in the process of national suicide." [42] Addressing a current controversial issue, if walls on our border help toward that goal (and all countries do have borders), then so be it and blessings upon our government for doing so!

Just as the Scriptures place the responsibility on government of moral preservation within its borders by the authority to "bear the sword," so it is true of it to protect its citizenry from evildoers' threats from without. "Just war" and its Biblical premises and principles have already been explored in chapter 1. It is enough to say for now, under the responsibility of government to preserve morality from threats outside of it, that, "on the matter of just warfare, it seems we can make appropriate references to support it by looking at the breadth of the New Testament material." [43]

The Biblical standard for God's people (that's you) to authoritatively speak and act toward government is that Christ and His Kingdom stand over society and her governments. As God's people, we are to expect from our government a submission before God as King, contractual fidelity to the Constitution, and moral preservation both within and without her borders. These responsibilities she has are positive values. However, we now turn to chapter 3 to address the boundaries of government and her authority, which are what God tells government they cannot do, and the role He expects us to play when we must resist government.

CHAPTER 3

Government's Lines in the Sand: Their Boundaries

To understand the solid foundation we are building, let me rehearse our method. We start from the Scriptures to build a Biblical ethic. From a Biblical ethic, we now have a Biblical worldview. From that Biblical worldview, we can rightly understand and speak to governmental boundaries and responsibilities. This is the point we are at.

I rehearse these steps because much of what we will now discover may seem surprising, shocking, or even radical. Therefore, it would do well for us to begin this investigation by having some Biblical exposition from a couple of texts. There are many we could draw from, but we will look primarily to a New Testament passage, Acts 4:7–31, with an additional documentation from an Old Testament passage, 2 Chronicles 26:16–22, to show the timelessness of these truths.

We will look at other passages as well, and those will be referenced; the Acts 4 passage is critical to explore because as Blaiklock states, "the Apostles, in these days of acute awareness and insight, were conscious that they were laying down principles for the Church. Their action, in fact, was to guide the Church through three (or was it nineteen?) centuries of persecution."[1] The passage in Chronicles simply exposes the consistency between the Old and New Testaments in dealing with this topic.

From these passages, we will see that first, governmental authority is to be respected (c. f. chapter 2). Second, governmental authority has its boundaries, and third, we are to oppose governmental authoritarianism (which will be stated in this chapter but further developed in chapter 4). Furthermore, applications from the Biblical texts will be applied to governments in general. However, the principle focus of application will be to the US Constitution and Declaration of Independence, since their derivation is clearly from an understanding of the Creator's Transcendent Law and set in the situational context of a Biblical map, as discussed earlier in chapter 2.

Early Warning: Our Respect for Governmental Authority Does Not Preclude Our Resistance

Listen clearly: an anti-authority spirit and an anti-government attitude is contrary to God as we saw in chapter 2. As we look at the passage in Acts, where Peter and John, and perhaps others, had been arrested for healing the lame beggar, we see an attitude of respect toward the authorities who had them arrested. They had remained silent and submissive up until they were addressed by the authorities to give an answer in Acts 4:7. *What seems perhaps un-notable at first glance but striking in the Greek text is how Peter respectfully addressed the governmental authorities in verse 7. This address is the giving to these leaders their full respect in their positions as Roman delegated authorities "rulers of the people," and their religious leadership "elders." It is critical to note that these religious leaders were sanctioned by Rome as their delegated, governmental authority, "collaborators of the Roman order,"[2], and, therefore, the analysis of these passages must account for their Roman governmental authority.* The general tenor of the entire address in Acts 4 is one of respectful address to both religious and governmental authority.

Although not as immediately clear, we see this similar respect given to King Uzziah in 2 Chronicles 26:16. Although King Uzziah was in the very act of defying God and His proper boundaries between the Kingship of Israel and the priesthood of Israel, the King was respectfully addressed. "It is not for you, Uzziah, to burn incense to the LORD." Although Uzziah was blatantly in defiance to YHWH and His Law, and although Azariah and his cadre of opposing men were at the ready and could have immediately taken physical action against Uzziah, instead, they gave the king a chance to save face and back down. However, as we shall see in the following verses, King Uzziah chose not to.

So before we proceed, one must note that a respectful attitude is the first disposition God's people and the citizens of a country, toward her government in whatever form it is. *Even the monumental work of Scottish pastor and theologian Samuel Rutherford, "Lex, Rex, or the Law and the Prince," which would cause a revolution across the world in governments, began with this very premise, "All civil government is immediately from God in its root."³*

However, respect for government does not preclude resistance against it. *The instructive passages of Romans 13 and 1 Peter 2: 13ff are fleshed out by those Apostles throughout the narrative passages of their lifestyle. We have seen clearly here in Acts 4, and in some manner 2 Chronicles 26, that a decision to defy authority in not lightly taken, but even in doing so, as we shall see, is done with humility. The citizen, and more pointedly, Christian citizens, are to have an attitude of respect for government. To not do so is to have "opposed the ordinance of God; and they who have opposed will receive condemnation upon themselves" (Rom. 13:2). This is to be the foundational attitude and disposition toward government. As we shall see though, respect and subjection to government is not unqualified.*

Governmental Authority, Biblical Boundaries, and Biblical Opposition to It

Keeping the respect starting point in mind, we will now look more closely at governmental boundaries and calling those boundaries out if they are crossed, and even opposing government if they do.

Peter and John had done nothing illegal in the healing of the lame beggar. They knew that; the rulers knew that. The key question to them in verse 7 was "In what power or in what name you did this?" That the miracle had taken place was beyond question, as the evidence was literally standing before them. *At most, some commentators state that this was an attempt, and a far stretch at that, to accuse the Apostles of magic prohibited by Deuteronomic Law (Deut. 13:1ff) and therefore to perhaps put them to death.* [4] In fact, the healing itself was not truly the crux of the clash of sphere boundaries between "Church and state" in this text.

Our instruction comes from how Peter answered their question of authority cited in verse 7 by referring to Jesus as the one in whose power and name they had healed the lame beggar. Get this: Peter had made a clear, unapologetic declaration of the Kingship of Jesus over the leaders he was addressing, and the miracle was a testimony to that fact. An even greater evidence pointed out was the resurrection of Jesus. These undisputed miraculous events were the source of their boldness. The council could not rebut the fact of the resurrection of Jesus, the King from whose authority Peter and John had healed the man before them. *"It is particularly striking that neither on this nor any other subsequent occasion did the Sanhedrin take any serious action to disprove the apostles' central affirmation—the resurrection of Jesus."* [5] It was only when "they commanded them not to speak or teach at all in the name of Jesus" (v. 18) that the Apostles drew the authority boundary and limitation of their governing rulers. They then give a Spirit-filled declaration from King Jesus to defy their government.

Noting carefully the content of how Peter responded to the prohibition in verse 18 within the Greek text is extremely telling, and exposes the clash for what it is. What Peter told the governmental and religious leader was, "Since indeed it is right before God to listen obediently to God rather than to you all, you first judge!" This is one of those cases of bad English but good Greek. To clarify in other words, Peter was instructing the governmental-religious leaders on the basics of legal jurisprudence, which put those leaders in a defenseless corner. It would be mutually agreed in that court that God's Law trumps man's law. Here Peter states that King Jesus's authority trumped their secular and religious authority and equated Jesus with God. The Apostles' mental conviction and soul's conscience before God could not be legislated against (and neither can yours), and they had committed no moral nor legal wrong before God in healing the lame man.

Furthermore those leaders knew too well that one's conscience to obey YHWH was primary above obedience to men and their laws. "If the point were to put these judges in the abstract, whether the command of God or a human commandment should be obeyed in the event of a clash between the two, they would have had no hesitation in affirming that the divine command must be obeyed at all costs." This conviction and conscience is what drove the Apostles and the early Church, and it is what should drive the Church today. This is the key to your personal gravity and perspective to be above others in clear discernment. What the leaders/legal authorities had commanded the Apostle to do was illegal in the sight of God, and the governmental-religious leaders had no legal argument and therefore no response to them except to "rattle their sabers" in an attempt to intimidate them. (Watch how often those in authority do this very thing when they're in the wrong and know it.)

In this historical context, these governmental judges had a Judeo background in law and knew the Scriptures; they could not argue against Peter's point. Unfortunately, most of today's governmental leaders do not have any philosophical training in the derivation of Law or jurisprudence, or if they do, have no respect for God and His Law as a transcendent premise.

Nonetheless, the reality remains, this truth stands: God is King over Law and authority. You must look at men's laws through the lens of God's Law. Specifically to the Apostles' argument, King Jesus and His Kingdom determine the Righteousness, or lack thereof, in man's laws. Government is God's institution, and He has set boundaries to man's governmental authority. What we learn from the Apostles and the early Church is that it is the responsibility of the Church, God's Kingdom agents, to boldly hold their governments to His standards of Law and government.

Although in a different historical context, we see this same trespassing of a sphere boundary in governmental authority in 2 Chronicles. God had designed a clear distinction between the monarchies of Israel from the priesthood of Israel. Uzziah, disillusioned by pride in his successful kingship, had envied the union of kingship and high priesthood of pagan nations around him. Despite knowing the law, he sought to trespass this boundary.[7] "It is not for you, Uzziah, to burn incense to the LORD, but for the priests, the sons of Aaron, who are consecrated to burn incense" (v. 18). The lesson is clear: God has set boundaries for all of His institutions, and to defy them only brings corruptive destruction, as the Hebrew text in verse 16 describes it.[8]

It is also instructive to note the contrasting attitude of government when it has forgotten its divine role. While the Apostles remained respectful in their disposition toward government, as did the priests before Uzziah, the governmental leadership arrogantly looked down upon those under their authority. Government leaders will "snob" you and your King when you correct them.

For example, in Acts, the questioning of the Apostles by the authorities begins with condescension. "There is scornful emphasis in the position of the pronoun—υμεισ at the end of verse 7: 'people like you',"[9] "-υμεισ: as if in scorn with depreciatory emphasis at the close of the question."[10] King Uzziah, in 2 Chronicles 26:16–19 first presumes to march right into the Temple with censor in hand as if, "he owned the place," even though he did not. Second, when firmly but respectfully countered by the priests, the king's reaction was, "Uzziah…was enraged." The very idea that he would be stopped by his "lowly" citizenry (and rightfully and legally so) was more than his prideful and presumptuous ego could handle: "I'm the boss and I'll make the rules; step aside peons!"

The pathology learned is this: boundary breaching by government leaders and the wrongful trespassing of government past its authorized role is a symptomatic result of their ignorance of, or arrogance over, their God-given limitations. When their illegal actions are questioned, they will simply belittle and disparage those questioning them. When questioned and held accountable, since they have no arguable response to truth or fact, all they can do is threaten with the only tool they have left: physical power. However, if met with equal or greater power, the government will tremble in fear, and well they should. This is precisely why our nation is in the state it is in. We have failed to defy, particularly, *en masse*, our government's ungodly laws and actions! Where did the backbone of God's people go?

The Biblical ethic or principle to live by is that governments have defined, specific roles from God, whose boundaries are not to be breached without destructive consequences to itself and her citizens. When government does so, the conviction and conscience of her citizens is to drive them to be respectful but to act with clear opposition and resistance against those leaders. The disposition of God's Kingdom and her citizens is to be on the offense, not the defense.

Why don't we see that today? What has happened to God's people of character who now tremble and fear their before their employee government? Why are we passive before government when we are called to be government's leaders and instructors that they are to fear?

Governmental Authoritarianism Must Be Resisted

Later within this book, we will delve further into our (read, "your") obligation and duty to resist authoritarianism. However, a brief sketch of that topic from the Biblical analysis at hand is foundational. Whenever governmental authorities have abused their proper domain and role before God's boundaries, they are guilty of authoritarianism. A classic definition of this word is this:

> **Authoritarianism,** *principle of blind submission to authority, as opposed to individual freedom of thought and action. In government, authoritarianism denotes any political system that concentrates power in the hands of a leader or small elite that is not constitutionally responsible to the body of the people.* Authoritarian leaders often exercise power

arbitrarily and without regard to existing bodies
of law.[11]

The last sentence in that definition is the key point that reflects
back to a Biblical principle for Law and government. When governmental leaders trespass their God-given boundaries, it becomes the
responsibility of the citizen to confront or even oppose that leadership. Those who are in God's Kingdom, since they know the God of
Law, have a moral obligation to take the lead. More about constitutional Law will be discussed in a later section.

In Acts 4:8–12, Peter and John stood before their governmental
leaders who had had them arrested and jailed overnight. Upon their
opening (and belittling) question fraught with baseless accusation,
Peter takes the offense, and not the defense, in their court of law.
"The apostles are technically on their defense, but actually they have
gone over to the attack."[12]

*Peter gives a synopsis of the authority and power of Jesus Christ
which implies His authority over the government leaders and provides
exhibit 1, the lame man standing before them, as evidence to that claim.
The Greek text is almost pointing to humor: "And here he is, still standing.". Furthermore, in a direct manner, Peter points the finger of inJustice
at the government, "whom you yourselves crucified, whom God raised"
(exhibit 2, the still, empty tomb), revealing God's reversal of the government's indictment and execution of Jesus as gross inJustice on their part.
This was not, "merely to remind them of their fault, but perhaps also they
might understand how vain it was to fight against God (Calvin)"[13]*

So Peter stands before these religious leaders, these delegated
Roman officials and, like the genre of an Old Testament prophet,
speaks for God in judgment against them. As will be discussed in
chapter 4, the Church has the obligation and authority before their
King (government officials) to take the prophetic role in confrontation to the Kingdom of men when that Kingdom trespasses their
boundaries.

The passage in Acts 4:13–18 tells us of the government's reaction to the apostles' actions. These government leaders were speech-
less and taken aback. They were used to people squirming in their

presence. (Like we do now?) Again the Greek text displays the utter perplexity of the Court.[14] No squirming cowardice from these men as the rulers "observed" their boldness (v. 13, a present participle depicting their ongoing observation of an unflinching disposition). With nothing to accuse them of and by their own admission fear of this truth spreading out of control (vv. 14–17), all they can do is threaten them further in verse 18.

In refusal to obey the dictum by the government, Peter calls the government to sanity before God first by a call to a reflection of Law before God ("You judge," v. 19). Secondly, these Church representatives in Court collectively defy their government's orders ("we cannot," v. 20). The essential lesson from these Scriptures is simply this: "Truth equals confrontation."[15] When called upon to defend truth, there will be a clash from those who oppose it. A respectful attitude as a premise, yes, but bold, unflinching, confrontation and opposition nonetheless.

Powerful lessons can be learned about abusive governments when they tread beyond God's boundaries for them. First, they cannot bear facts and truths that point to their guilt. All they can do is rattle their sabers (v. 21), hoping to drown out the indictment against them. (Today's version is seeing far left liberals shouting and yelling inane, emotional words, disallowing any logical discussion) Second, and more importantly, the Church is intended to be a force to be reckoned with. Boldness with truth and confidence in the face of government leaves their leaders in fear (vv. 16–17). Governments should have a healthy fear of their citizens as well. The Church is to take the lead in that, as noted earlier.

This same reality can be seen in 2 Chronicles 26. When the King marched in to tread past his authority, he was met face-to-face with the priest and eighty "valiant men" (v. 17). They "stood in the way of Uzziah" (v. 18) to forcibly (with lethal arms) prevent him from trespassing his role. "The number and character of the helping priests was so that they could do their work promptly with an imposing force."[16] All the king could do (for he knew he was wrong) was to go into a kingly fit of rage, his version of "saber rattling" (v.19). Before bloodshed could occur in this clash of *government vs. God* boundaries, God stepped in with miraculous and immediate judgment: "leprosy broke out on his forehead" (v. 19). Eighty-plus courageous men basically threw the king out because he had defied God the King, and they simply cooperated with God in his judgment by doing so. King Uzziah offered no resistance to God or His representatives with their forceful judgment (v. 20).

I have a disturbing question for you from these texts of Scripture: were these priests and were the Apostles in these Biblical accounts guilty of treason against their government? Answer: no. Instead they were simply submitting to God's government and God's jurisdiction when their earthly governments had stepped out of their God-ordained roles. If there was treason against the government, it was the government leaders who were guilty of treason before God and man.

By contrast, these resistors were in a righteous stance before God and man. We must learn a critical lesson here: It does not matter what those leaders then perceived or what the public then might perceive of these so-called rebels against government. In our contemporary application, we might add, it does not matter what the media might portray the militant Church as. Nor does it matter what those who are cowardly and passive in the Church and her leaders perceive either as they glibly quote verses from the Bible without context. Respectful resistance and confrontation against evil is God's will for His Kingdom citizens. If family, neighbors, friends, or fellow Church members disagree, they disagree in ignorance, irresponsibility, or even cowardice. You must answer to God, not people, however close they might be. You and I are not called by our triumphant King to be irresponsible cowards!

Constitutional Boundaries of Government under God

Now, what does God say from these Biblical texts to governmental constitutions? What is the nature of a constitution, and what does this have to do with God? First, government is God's idea and is therefore under God's accountability and morality. Second, contracts, covenants, and constitutions fall under God's jurisdiction of accountability and morality.

I am greatly indebted to Dr. Loren Lomasky from the University of Virginia as his writings shed much light on the legal bases of government formations. In particular, I will quote at length from his paper entitled "Contract, Covenant, and Constitution," submitted to George Mason University. The purpose of very briefly discussing the political science aspect of government formation in a theological study is because of the relationship between Law and theology.

We have already established that government is a creation of God. We now turn to those theories of governmental structure that formed our country and the moral obligations the government has before God to keep those agreements made with the citizens of a country. Those theories and legal foundations are contract, covenant, and constitution.

The Nature of the US Constitution as a Contract

Since the focus of this book is to form an informed Biblical base upon which to understand government, we will center in on the applications from law rather than upon the great intricacies of legal theory. The idea of "social contract" is that government forms from the people up to the formation of a government. It is a "bottom up" government that begins with the people to form a government for themselves. Within the social contract the citizens are not property of, nor inferior to, their rulers. In fact, the state is in service to the citizens. The state owes the citizens her contracted obligations. Should the regime formed by the people fail to perform agreed upon obligations, they are to be cast off and dismissed. This arrangement allows a dignity and value of the citizens that is of no less than the King or their respected leaders. The government and her citizens share a mutual and healthy fearful respect of one another. The Constitution of the United States was constructed by the Founding Fathers with the social contract much in mind, yet not exclusively.[17]

When the Constitution of the United States was constructed, it was done with a Biblical milieu and a largely Biblical consensus in mind, as pointed out in chapter 1. However, as we have seen in the previous Biblical texts, the transcendent foundation to Law and government applies to all governments, not just the United States, as Christ is King over the entire cosmos (Matthew 28:18).

There are responsibilities to and boundaries from her citizens that God expects government to keep. One of those is the responsibility to keep and hold contract (social contract in this case) honestly and faithfully: "If a man vow a vow unto the LORD, or swear an oath to bind his soul with a bond; he shall not break his word, he shall do according to all that proceedeth out of his mouth" (Num. 30:2, KJV). "He despised the oath in breaking the covenant, and behold, he gave his hand and did all these things; he shall not escape" (Ez. 17:18, KJV). Two of the six things listed of what God hates in Proverbs 16 are a "lying tongue" and a "false witness," both of which apply to contract or covenant. Have you noticed that government officials (and Law enforcement and military personnel) take "oaths of office"? These are made before God and the citizens of government (Yep, that's right, just YouTube one for an example).

The God-given boundary is that a government cannot breach or break that contract. A country's constitution, particularly the Constitution of the United States for our purpose here, is such an example:

> *The American government was established with the understanding that such transcendent values would affect what otherwise is simply a social contract. When the state forgets or denies those values that were the original conditions of the contract, in essence it abrogates its contract with its citizens. It is then that the Church must take the initiative and call the state into account.*[18]

Abrogation *means to abolish a Law or contract by authoritative action; or what I have called "authoritarianism."* For the state, the

77

Congress, the Supreme Court, the White House, or any other governmental entity to do so is to rebel against God Himself and to
act as a traitor to its citizens. **When the state does so, they should
expect confrontation and resistance from her citizens for their
moral breach against God and Country. They have displaced God
and are attempting to take His seat on the throne.** "When a state
claims divine honors, there will always be warfare between Christ and
Caesar, for two rival gods claim the same jurisdiction over man." [19]

The Nature of the US Constitution as a Covenant

The US Constitution, however, has more than one parent. The
social contract gave legitimacy to an authoritative institution because
it was by the consent of the governed. However, the annals of history
show that the idea of consent by the governed goes even further back
to the history of Israel in the idea of covenant. The term used in the
foundations of Israel's government was *covenant* in Hebrew.

*Although there were many "covenants" in the Hebrew Scriptures,
the shining star is the Sinaitic covenant. Within two months of Israel's
miraculous deliverance from Egypt by God, culminating in the Red Sea
crescendo, God had Moses gather the elders. There, the proposal by God
is that He will offer His laws to them as long as they swear allegiance
and consent to be governed by Him. The people agreed to this covenantal
government relationship with YHWH by saying, "Whatever the LORD
has said, we will do" (Ex. 19:7–8).*

*The legal actualities were all present; the year and date of occur-
rence, parties identified (the "house of Jacob"), the central figures witnessing to the covenant (Moses, Aaron, and "the LORD your God who
brought you out of the land of slavery"), and the terms of the covenant
in great detail. "The relationship, then, is held to be genuinely mutual,
incorporating specific performances from both parties." [20] The greater distinction between contract and covenant is that it is much more personal,
embedding relationships into what would be otherwise mere contract.
"Not just the nation's well-being but its very existence is a function of the
Sinai undertaking. It means that Israel will thenceforth not only have a*

collection of biographies but a history. The covenant is a charter for com-munal achievement."[21] Many of the key elements to both contract and covenant come together in the idea of constitution, particularly when it comes to the Constitution of the United States.

Again keep this clearly in mind for those who are ignorant of understanding these matters. It is obvious our Founding Fathers were not seeking to establish some kind of theocracy. Instead, they were simply seeking to borrow sacred principles of government from the Sinaitic Covenant. The whole idea of honoring governmental cove-nant was the background to the colonists who founded the United States. It was the breaking of such a covenant by King George before God and the people that gave the colonists their moral indignation for war with Great Britain. It would also be the covenantal basis that they would ensure into the later constitution of the United States.

> Two principles enunciated in *Lex Rex* were drawn up by the colonists in declaring their indepen-dence from Great Britain in 1776. First, there was the concept of the covenant or the constitution between the ruler and God and the people. This covenant, Rutherford argued, could not grant the state absolute or unlimited power without violat-ing God's law. Taking the cue from Rutherford the colonists asserted that King George had vio-lated his covenant with God by transgressing their God-given rights…which was later written into the Declaration of Independence.[22]

The Nature of the US Constitution as a Constitution

Constitution shares in the same elements that both contract and covenant have to bring political outcomes by means of mutual consent. Whereas the social contract tends to be a strictly objective, legal agreement, and whereas covenant brings relational dimension to a contractual agreement between God, citizens and government, constitutional government (in particular, of the United States) is a hybrid of these two parents, delicately interlocking the two:

> *Let me try to be clear about what I take the significance of covenant to be for the understanding of the functionality of constitutionalism. It has often been observed that Americans treat their founding documents as having quasi-religious status. I have argued that the Biblical narrative of covenant is undeniably theological but also intrinsically political. It presents a theory of institutional justification for which consent is a necessary condition. That renders it (the Constitution of the U.S.) uniquely suitable as an alternative to social contract for modeling a polity for citizens who are bound by Law yet also free.[23]*

The discussion of contract, covenant, and constitution by political scholars—such as Lomasky and Whitehead—is critical to understanding the uniqueness to the United States Constitution. Although not a religious document per se, the political academicians only bolster the Biblical map and compass of the US Constitution, as I have argued for in chapter 1. It was the totality of the people before God and man who would "ordain and establish" the union. It was the totality of the people who sought God to charter and bless their path into the unknown future. "Just as the covenant at Sinai is the gold standard of covenants, the constitution of the United States of America is the gold standard of constitutionalism."[24] Government is to be morally responsible before God, the King. They are also to be legally responsible to their citizens and to God, the King.

Before we leave this overview of contract, covenant, and constitution, a direct theological application should be made. The Church, God's people, is Christ's Kingdom citizens because of covenant. The fulfilled blood covenant in Jesus Christ was anticipated in all earlier anticipatory covenant(s) detailed in the Scriptures of the Old Testament. Please follow this: as anticipated in the governmental covenant at Mount

Sinai between God and Israel, so now we, the Church have a ful-filled governmental covenant between God and His Church. We are not like Israel who had a singular governmental citizenship before God because we today, in God's plan, we all have two citizenships. First, we have a primary governmental citizenship (God's Kingdom in Christ), and second, we have a governmental citizenship to the country in which we live. This must be perfectly clear: the Christian has one foot of unchangeable loyalty in King Jesus and another foot in responsible yet conditional loyalty to their earthly, governmental leaders. *The paradigm of loyalty goes far beyond mere individual and simplistic ideals of morality which will come in conflict;* you, the Kingdom citizens, are to speak and act to the very system of government itself. Although many of these foundational truths you are learning can be applied to any government and her people, it is with even greater gravity that we now investigate government's restrictions and the consequences of constitutional breach. What are the consequences of government acting bad?

Fighting Words: Governmental Breach and Consequences That Should Happen

All government officials are required to take an oath of office to uphold the Constitution, as described in articles II and VI of the US Constitution. It reads, with some minor variation at times, as follows:

> *I, [name], do solemnly swear (or affirm) that I will support and defend the*
> *Constitution of the United States against all enemies, foreign and domestic; that I will bear true faith and allegiance to the same; that I take this obligation freely, without any mental reservation or purpose of evasion; and that I will well and faithfully discharge the duties of the office on which I am about to enter. So help me God.*[25]

Yet listen to the betrayal of this oath by a Supreme Court Justice, Charles Evan Hughes, sworn into office with that very oath, who would say, "The Constitution is what the judges say it is."[26] This example is but a small sampling of an overwhelming tide of the attitude that many government officials hold. These government officials see themselves as the authority to the making, interpretation, and execution of Law in direct contradiction to the Constitution they swore to uphold. *They have become "Rex Lex," "the king is law," and elevated themselves to kings opposed to the foundational basis of the Constitution of "Lex Rex," "the Law is King" (that is, God's Law).*

This is not a new problem. Rutherford's treatise by that very title above, Lex Rex, *became the springboard of government revolution from Scotland, all across Europe, and was taken up by our Constitutional Fathers. This attitude of Rex Lex is precisely what the colonists accused King George of in the Declaration of Independence as a "long train of abuses and usurpations...to reduce them to absolute Despotism" and which caused them to "throw off such a government."*

Are you hearing this? The very disgust you have toward what has happened to your government which has elevated itself above you, and above God, is the very same disgust that led to people who would eventually start this country. You fellow citizens are not alone historically and you are not alone now! According to Rutherford's Biblical-political analysis in *Lex Rex*, which had so heavily influenced the political world at that time, man's Law must be derived from God's revelation. The Colonists saw King George's evolving laws against their colonies as a violation of that premise, and therefore illegitimate, and therefore not "law" at all.

Today, many officials and leaders within government have removed the Transcendent Lawgiver who is above man from the basis of law, and have forsaken the roots of the Constitution and create illegitimate laws and illegally try to enforce them! This is a Biblical, legal, and moral breach on their part. *"The removal of the transcendent sucks meaning from the law. With no ultimate reference point supporting it Law can only be enforced by the bayonet. So the state seeks more and more coercive power."*[27]

Please! Step back and look at our current political and cultural battle! This battle, this war is on! A milestone of education for us is the following: Those government officials who are guilty of authoritarianism want no competition to their "bayonet," as Colson puts it, and therefore despise the Second Amendment, which was meant to arm the citizenry against their despotism. Listen to this, please! The "right to bear arms" in the Second Amendment was placed there to protect the people against their government if it went awry, not to give citizens a right to protect themselves against criminals which is already a God-given right. Only a fool would say this war is not presently going on? What will you do about it? What will we, as the Church triumphant, do about it?

I have used the term authoritarianism *to define "governmental leaders who have chosen to exercise power without regard to God's Law, or constitutional law, or both." Those actions by those leaders are breach with God, the Constitution, and her citizens. The Founders saw the high possibility of a federal authoritarianism growing. James Madison, in The Federalist, no. 45, would write, "The powers delegated by the proposed Constitution to the federal government are few and defined. Those which remain in the state governments are numerous and indefinite."[28]*

I quoted the skewed perspective of a Supreme Court Justice earlier. Thomas Jefferson warned of such abuses by the Court when he said,

> *Nothing in the Constitution has given them [the Supreme Court] a right to decide the Executive, more than the Executive to decide for them. The opinion which gives the judges the right to decide what laws are constitutional and what not, not only for themselves in their own sphere of action, but for Legislative and Executive also, in their spheres, would make the judiciary a despotic branch.[29]*

Abraham Lincoln would later echo the same warning in his first inaugural address: "If the policy of the Government...is to be irrevocably fixed by decisions of the Supreme Court...the people will have ceased to be their own rulers, having to that extent practically resigned their Government into the hands of that eminent tribunal."[30] That predicted nightmare has come to pass decades ago, and has only increased. Sociological Law has replaced God's Transcendent Law so that Justice and Law have become the creations of the state. The Supreme Court has set themselves up as the ultimate interpreter of the Constitution, convoluting it far from its Biblical milieu. Legisprudence (what is legal as defined by the state) has become the norm rather than jurisprudence (what is "just" before God).

As the state via the SCOTUS (Supreme Court of the United States) interprets law, human children are the creation of the state, and the state therefore has the power of life and death over the unborn. The state then creates new liberties and rights for a woman to slaughter her child. God and the Bible no longer belong in jurisprudence. Is this grounds to be angry enough to fight? I would say both as a theologian and a learned patriot, a father, and a husband that the answer is a resounding yes!

Within this illegitimate map of authoritarianism in defiance to the Biblical map of the Constitution, the state finds their greatest threat in God's Kingdom agents, who have the authority to confront them. Ask yourself: How much of a threat are we now? Are we ready to stand up to their presumptuous bullying? Both you who have Biblical convictions (and even worse) are trained and responsibly armed, are those despots' greatest enemy. You are also the enemy of a lawless or anarchist culture (take the Antifa movement, for example). The "authoritarian spirit" and lawless rioters therefore despise the First and Second Amendments and twists them in an attempt to make the voice of Law impotent, "rattling their sabers" in threats against the Christian Church.

Kimberly Strassel of the *Wall Street Journal* documents and describes how the US government has openly and unashamedly cooperated in targeting conservative groups and Churches that have been exercising their First Amendment rights, and representing "tens of thousands of Americans." She details criminal actions by the government using a three-step process of harassment, trumped investigation and prosecution, and blackmail that has proven successful in shutting down entire groups or individuals.[31]

Since I began the writing of this book, it is now a bygone conclusion that the IRS, by their own admission, sought to silence conservative groups by unfairly targeting these voices (Reuters, October 26, 2017). However, despite the skewed claims of modern-day authoritarians, the First Amendment, along with the rest of the Bill of Rights, was birthed in a Christian theological environment. *Thomas Jefferson himself would concede this point as he admitted that it was a Princeton theologian who heavily influenced the Bill of Rights, "the fact is unquestionable that the Bill of Rights was drawn originally by George Mason."*[32]

The purpose of the First Amendment was two-fold. First, that there would be no established national Church for the united thirteen states, or a "Church of the United States" like the "Church of England" from their estranged motherland. James Madison articulated this purpose of the Amendment: "the people feared one sect might obtain preeminence, or two combine together, and establish a religion to which they would compel others to conform."[33]

The second purpose was that the state was not to impede or to interfere with the free practice of religion, the exact opposite of what is claimed and practiced today. Today, both government and the media have used a deceitful lie of "separation of Church and state" to silence the Church rather than to allow its flourishing and cultural seasoning. They have been successful in largely caging you, that ferocious lion. Colson sums up the state agenda as an attempt to privatize religion so that it has no relationship to one's moral behavior and, I would add, no longer be a threat to the state.[34]

For now, I will delay a Christian view of the Second Amendment of the citizenry's right to bear arms in protection against a tyrannical government until a later study in chapter 4. However, a closing note on government breach and consequences should be stated. Robert George, Professor of Jurisprudence at Princeton University, goes on record on the growing tyranny of the Federal Government and laments, "We've drifted a long way from the original vision of the Founders," and warns the public that "Freedom can be taken away, but it can also be given away by sheer ignorance."[35]

The government has boundaries. When the government breaches those boundaries, it is the citizen's duty to be an educated and informed force to counter the wrongs committed. Even popular Christian magazines are heralding that call: "But no one who confesses that Jesus Christ is Lord can meekly submit to the proposition that man-made laws are sacred and inviolable. We need to restore a bold willingness to treat principled resistance as a live possibility, rather than a relic of a bygone era."[36] What form should that principled resistance take? Civil disobedience against unrighteous laws of government? How about armed defense against Antifa (for example) threats to grave bodily harm or fear of death?

The government should expect no less of her citizens. Like Peter and John before the Law court, and like the wall of priests before a defying king Uzziah, the Church needs to rise again as that voice and force that the government would be afraid to reckon with. Government should expect massive civil disobedience against inJustice, as God defines it. Government officials should expect outright defiance to illegitimate laws they pass. The government should fear bloodshed and forceful responses when citizens justly defend their lives and property against a culture bent on lawlessness! Government courts should be just as confounded at the unflinching boldness of modern-day Peters and Johns. Citizens, especially God's Kingdom citizens, need to make a history making decision of whose side they are on. You, the reader, must make that decision before your King. The Psalmists did: "Can wicked rulers be allied with you, those who frame inJustice by statute?" and "For kingship belongs to the LORD, and he rules over the nations" (Psalm 94:20 and 22:28, ESV).

I, for one, swear allegiance to the kingship of the LORD first and above all. How about you? Which side do you choose? Will you join those who have chosen to leave a legacy rather than an unremarkable life? Will you join forces with many who are convinced to their bones that they must fight, or be cowards for having not been men and women of God? If you are reading this far, I think we know which one you are.

CHAPTER 4

Citizen Lines in the Sand:
Your Shocking Responsibilities

F air warning: This chapter calls Christians to "grow up" and to be the men and women God has called them to be. If this is offensive to you, take it up with your King, not with me. We will look, in a Biblical nutshell, what your responsibilities are toward government. This should surprise you, and these words are "fighting words" against a culture which despises these basic truths.

If you were to peruse the typical book on this subject, they will address Christians as to how God instructs them in their ethical behavior toward society and government. Instead, we will look at the same subject through a different lens. We will take the position of how the Christian should use God's will in this area to inform and instruct our society and our governments. Are you ready to learn these? You, the heavenly citizen, as an emissary from the Supreme Governor, are to be the instructor to earthly governments and your culture. Here we will educate you, the Christian, so that you can be responsible tutors toward society and government on the critical doctrine of "The Citizen's Responsibilities to Their Government." The education of the Christian in this realm of politics is desperately needed. Charles Colson laments,

> "In the Kingdom of God one learns the obligations
> of citizenship from the Scriptures, the ultimate

> source of basic Christian truth. Unfortunately, most people, Churched or unChurched, are woefully ignorant in this area. The first responsibility for the citizen of the Kingdom, then, is to understand historic Christian truth: to know Scripture and the classic fundamentals of the faith."[1]

The following Biblical "mini-studies," based upon solid research, are meant to begin that Christian education so that all citizens will have a platform with which to speak to their government with God's authority. Please don't miss the point that means you. The following is meant to give you the spiritual tenacity to stand tall for God based upon the solid foundation of Scripture. You are to speak on behalf of God to your government and culture, like countless millions of your fellow Christians throughout history. The foundation on which these truths are extracted come primarily from the highlights of a summary analysis of Mark 12:28–30 (c.f. Matthew 22:34–40).

Biblical Foundation

In order to understand the primary responsibilities a Christian citizen has to his government, or his king, as it were, we will look at the King of king's statement about the primary responsibility one has to Him, and work from the greater Kingdom of God argument to the lesser human government application. When Jesus was asked on at least one occasion in Mark 12:28–30 (c.f. Matthew 22:36), "What commandment is foremost of all?" He gave a timeless response that set the pattern that has informed families, cultures, and governments of their relationships to one another for centuries.

What Jesus was actually asked here was (from the Greek text), "What sort of commandment is of greatest significance?"[2], *"ποια, it is a question, not of an individual commandment but of characteristic quality."[3] In less technical words,* Jesus was being asked for a broad Biblical interpretive basis with which to understand God's will for man—a request for a view of the forest to understand the trees and leaves and roots within that forest. Whatever direction you seek from God in life, if you are seeking His will on a matter, this paradigm is your starting point. Will we then apply it to our particular question at hand.

Jesus, in response to this question, states the controlling disposition to His citizens, His people, for all life, all families, all cultures, all societies and all governments for all time: "You shall love the Lord your God with all your heart, and all your mind, and with all your soul, and with all your strength…" (v. 30). Here is the essential formula for relational health, including that of society and government: citizens are to love God first! No relationship can come first before our utter devotion and love for God. Government is not the focus of our attention nor the head of our priorities. If there is dissension in relationships, the triage prescription is "Love the Lord your God." If there is conflict between our government that challenges our obedience, love, and devotion for God, we choose God over government.

As we sojourn through the forest of life and wander through the trees and leaves of man's laws, we must always keep our heads and hearts in view of God's forest. Learn this following critical truth from God: We must be informed of government laws, but they are not our ultimate guide for our behavior and choices. What is right before God and man, as God dictates it, is that standard to which we submit. If it is a costly choice, we remain steadfast because we love Him with all of our being, "with the whole [repeated three times] of our heart, soul, and mind."

But let's view that prescription from the King's lips as about more than the negative inevitable conflicts. These words from Jesus are about positive prevention and redemption for us, our culture and our government. This prescription from Jesus is the medicinal balm to preserve peace and wholeness in one's self and in our society. When God's citizens love Him first, the "Kingdom of God invades the stream of history, it breaks the vicious and otherwise irreversible cycles of violence, inJustice and self-interest. In this way the Kingdom of God equips its citizens, as Augustine said, to be the best citizens in the Kingdoms of man."[4] The inevitable consequence of our making

God first in our love for Him is the positive effects for society and for government.

Jesus doesn't stop there, though. He then goes on to say, "The second is this…," or, as Matthew puts it, "and the second is the same" (v. 39). It appears that Jesus interconnects these two commandments with heavenly glue. *"δευτερα …this second is declared like to the first… amounts to the same thing = the second is also a great, first commandment, being though formally subordinate to the first, really the first in another form: love to God and love to man one."5 Another scholar repeats this grammatical analysis: "The first and second…are inseparable. A wholehearted love for God necessarily finds its expression in a selfless concern for another man which decides and acts in a manner consistent with itself."6* "You shall love God…You shall love your neighbor" (vv. 29, 31). "The whole duty of man, the whole moral-spiritual law, can be summed up in one word: love."7

The following precept I use often and so many of my students remember, as you must remember: "A text without a context becomes a pretext." By themselves, these verses can be taken out of context to exalt a false Christianity based upon a grossly twisted version of God's love. For the purposes of this manual, we will remain true to the heart of these verses to instruct us on our responsibility to government and society. Love for God is foremost. Love for self and neighbor are to follow dogmatically. Hang in here with me, as we look at all Jesus stated in these crucial verses.

Although I don't want to bore you with grammatical analysis of the Greek text, humor me for a moment at this critical juncture. The critical phrase "As yourself" is often missed altogether, but is paramount in understanding responsibility toward society and government. "As yourself" gives the prioritization of whom to love. With the comparative particle "as" in the indicative mood, the second clause, "as yourself." is a descriptive phrase of how the first should be conducted.8

Love yourself properly so you can love your neighbor properly. The way one loves oneself becomes the description of how to love one's neighbor. Within the larger context, one learns to properly love themselves in their loving of God.

A simple summarization of proper love from Jesus's quintessential formula is, in my paraphrase from the original text, this: "Love God with your whole being, first and foremost. Therefore, you learn to love yourself properly in this relational context with God. You therefore can love your neighbor be it wife, children, friend, culture (or government) properly as you've learned real, pure love from God."

An airline attendant dictates this same formula when she tells us adults that in case of an emergency, we are to place the oxygen mask on one's own face first, then to assist the child (or feeble person) with their oxygen mask. One can only assist or love another when one is able and functional. If one does not love oneself properly, one cannot properly love others. To the degree one's love for self is healthy (in the context of God's love) one can love and mentor healthy love to their neighbor, society, and government.

Summarized in a formula for you to memorize, those two commands would be (1) Love God passionately with your whole being, (2) Love yourself as God loves you, and (3) Love your neighbor as you love yourself. This sets the context for how one is to be responsible to society and government.

One final note to these preliminary notes on a Biblical foundation is to state an obvious assumption that should still be pointed out. When dealing with the greatest commandment as a basis for all relationships and extrapolating it to your citizen responsibility to government, it is assumed that the background to all conduct is premised upon Righteousness, as God defines it. Moral behavior and ethical conduct is a foundational basis to the discussion of relational responsibility. In fact, the Hebrew word used in Scripture Righteousness *implies much more than mere outward behavior. It also supplies the contextual meaning behind the New Testament word* Righteousness. *Within the Old Testament genre, Righteousness implied not mere legal, ethical behavior ("We must obey the Ten Commandments"), but rather relationship fulfillment from the heart ("Love the LORD thy God")[9] that prompted outward, legal, and proper behavior.[10] In other words, "love" by God's definition looks like He defines it, it includes "Justice" and "Righteousness" as He has colored it. We don't define "love" and all that means for us and others; love looks like how He sees it. (This writer has a paper submitted to Southwestern Baptist Theological Seminary entitled "Righteousness in the Old Testament" that supplies a deeper analysis on this subject and is available upon request.) With that explanation, it is only assumed that a citizen's responsibility to their government is set within the context of a "righteous" life (which is not a "holier than thou" life).*

Do not forget: Your first responsibility to government and society is to love God, love yourself, and to love your neighbor as yourself. But how does that practically play out in life? The explanation is simpler and nobler than you might think.

Your First Responsibility to Government: Life and Property Provision

First, Take Care of Yourself

One of the principal ways one is to love one's self is to take the responsibility of sustaining one's self financially, and to provide for one's own shelter and basic needs—in other words, to work and to own property. "Life and property provision" here in this section means that your basic biological necessities and means with which to nurture physical life and care are your responsibility.

The Apostle Paul becomes our instructor on these matters. I will quote several passages from him in different contexts. "But we exhort you brethren to mind your own affairs, and to work with your own hands, as we charged you; so that you may command the respect of outsiders, and be dependent on nobody" (1 Thess. 4:11–12). "For no man ever hates his own flesh, but nourishes it and cherishes it" (Eph. 5:29). "For you yourselves know how you ought to follow our example, because we did not act in an undisciplined manner among you, nor did we eat anyone's bread without paying for it, but with toil and labor we worked night and day, that we might not burden any of you." (2 Thess.3:7–8). "For even when we were with you, we used to give you this order: if anyone is not willing to work, then he is not to eat, either" (v. 10).

You can see that God's command to care for one's own needs runs directly contrary to the "entitlement" mentality that runs rampant in our culture. No one "owes you" anything. By the way, as you read these verses, did you also catch a glimpse of how contrary God's view is against so many premises in Socialism and current political voices?

Perhaps these passages seem merely as duty, but the essence behind work described here comes from a joy and privilege given to humankind by God. After the LORD had created the universe in five days, on the sixth day He then creates male and female in His image, unique from all other creation (Gen. 1:27). What follows is His directive to mimic Him in His work, to display the *imago dei,* "image of God," *by* cultivating and ruling over creation through labor. All this takes place *before* the Fall in the Garden and the consequent Curse (vv. 28–31). For any human being to retain their human dignity, they must participate in the dignity God has given them in their privilege to work and to rule. "When you shall eat of the fruit of your hands, you will be happy and it will be well with you" (Psalm 128:2).

Many, especially within the poorer demographics, have become entirely dependent upon government and society for their living needs (and wants). Such persons strip themselves of their God-given dignity by refusing to become productive citizens. Furthermore, when such people do so, they choose to live in a dysfunctional relationship with a socialist-leaning, codependent government, thereby producing all varieties of societal malaise and crime across our Country. The solution to so much of this is the recovery of self-dignity within our culture by their being instructed into becoming self-sustaining individuals and family units.

The citizen's (Christian or otherwise) first responsibility toward government is to be a responsible citizen who works to sustain themselves, to profit from their labor, and to flourish through their labor. The person who is able to work but does not, not only strips themselves of the human dignity God gave them but also wrongfully becomes a dependent upon others and society. "In a socialist type of society, it is easy to forget that society does not owe the able a living; rather it owes him an opportunity to make a living." [11]

This same Judeo-Christian "work ethic" and property ownership was formative in the (non-socialist) formations of the United States. *William Blackstone was an eighteenth-century jurist whose publication "Commentaries on the Law of England" set the standard for England, the early Colonies, and, later, the United States as a Judeo-Christian base for our law. Whitehead sums up Blackstone's Biblical basis of property ownership in early America:* "Blackstone argued that the cultural mandate given to Adam and Eve in Genesis 1 is the basis for man's possession of property. This divine mandate was the only true basis for the right to hold private property or, for that matter, any right." [12]

Rev. Prof. Samuel Rutherford was a Scottish Presbyterian pastor, theologian, and author whose formidable work based upon Biblical ethics *Lex Rex* became the cornerstone of what the proper relationship was to be between men and government. He wrote, "The natural liberty of man is to be free from any superior power on earth, and not to be under the will or legislative authority of man, but only to have the Law of nature for his rule." [13]

Upon reflection of Rutherford's statement, Samuel Adams wrote, "Among the natural rights of the colonists are these: first, a right to life; second, to liberty; third, to property." [14] These three, known as "Locke's Triad"—life, liberty, and property—became the foundation for basic rights of humanity before God that government was to protect. It was such a foundation for moral preservation that when it was originally written into the Declaration of Independence, the word *property* was to be reworded by Jefferson as, "the pursuit of happiness," so as to not confuse slaves as property in the issue. [15]

Carl F. H. Henry eloquently states this God-given honor of self-independence through labor: "He was to govern nature in order to develop to the full its potential for reflecting the glory of God and promote the well-being of man. Nature bore by creation and preservation the impress of the Divine Mind. Man is not to work independently of God." [16] Do you see the chain of thinking that led from Scriptures to our founding documents? These are critical ideas that were, and are, the foundations of why generations, including yours, have enjoyed the freedoms in the United States. Do you also see our culture's current thinking that are grossly contrary to God's ways of prosperity and peace? You must understand and exercise them to fulfill your responsibility to government under your Heavenly King.

To sum up God's statement of first responsibility a citizen has toward their government and society, it is their mandate to love one's self by reflecting the divine image of work and creating and producing and buying and selling and owning. This first responsibility and privilege is not narcissistic, however (as a proper love of self is learned in the context of one's love for God). From one's proper love of self stems a proper love for one's neighbor, namely, and first, for one's family.

Second, Take Care of Your Neighbor 1

If you have followed this trail properly, you have already concluded from the Biblical texts above that, from God's point of view, we are to love our neighbor as our self. There is a prioritization as to who our neighbor is. Paul would state to the young pastor Timothy, "If any one does not provide for his own, and especially those of his own household, he has denied the faith and is worse than an unbeliever" (1 Tim. 5:8). It is instructive to see how Paul prioritizes one's own family above others with the Greek adverb meaning "above all else." The provision for one's own household comes first above other "neighbors," if you would. In verse 16, he will further iterate the priority of families caring for their own widows so that the Church would not be "burdened" unnecessarily and could focus time and resources on widows who had no family.

The first=class conditional phrase, "If anyone does not provide," points to the affirmation of the reality. Indeed the early Church had those who were not providing properly for their families, and so Paul categorizes them as "*worse than* an unbeliever." "There are children, dependents, widows, orphans, and other indigent people. If any of these happens to be in one's immediate family or among his relatives, then it is his social responsibility to provide for them."[17] Therefore, one whose citizenship is with God's Kingdom (and I trust that is you) is to prioritize his own family in providing for them second only to properly caring for oneself. The same prioritization is equally true and applicable for any citizen in any government. Therefore, a citizen's first responsibility to their government is to be a productive, self-sustaining citizen, and secondly to provide the same for their family members. Of course, it is a foregone conclusion that those family members who are able within that family system learn and practice this same ethic.

I observed a beautiful display of this truth when I was investigating Cambodia as a possible ministry opportunity. At the time, the nation had a 45 percent HIV rate, according to the World Health Organization. One can only imagine how many cases of fully developed AIDS were ravaging the country, and it was an epidemic sweeping Cambodia. However, I had heard of an American missionary nurse who had opened an AIDS care center near Kampuchea, Cambodia. I sought to personally observe what I assumed, based on those statistics, would be a large facility handling hundreds or thousands of AIDS victims.

When I arrived, I observed a modest building about the size of a home. They had six beds, half of which were empty. Shocked, I asked the director, "Nurse Nancy," how it was in a country so decimated by AIDS that she had empty beds and only three patients. She responded, "Well, in this country, families take care of their own. If someone contracts AIDS, their family takes them in and cares for them to the end. These three here have absolutely no family at all, which is an extreme rarity here."

Since visiting Cambodia, I have called it the "Dark Country" because of its poverty, corruption, and hopelessness for time and eternity. However, at that moment, I stood shocked in front of Nurse Nancy to see that even in a "Dark Country" that had no Judeo-Christian basis, the *imago dei* could shine forth and instruct the world around them of God's truth and instruction, without them even realizing it. The Church (Nurse Nancy and her ministry organization) there had only to take care of those who were "widows indeed," as it were, because the culture around it had had it ingrained into them that family is to be provided for, no matter how poor the circumstances or how distant the family tie was. There are no government programs there to provide food stamps or housing, so the masses all work, however meagerly, to care for themselves and their families, even unto death. Our American culture at the very least, has much to learn in this particular area from a largely pagan culture, and needs to relearn from and reenact our Judeo-Christian roots of this responsibility to God and our government. Family is "neighbor 1." "Neighbor 2" is the Body of Christ.

Third, Take Care of Neighbor 2

If you look at the "neighbor" priorities, you will observe a concentric circle pattern. The innermost circle is your immediate family. The next circle is the Body of Christ. A listing of a few passages bears testimony to the Body of Christ as being the next concentric circle. "So then, while we have opportunity, let us do good to all men, and especially to those who are of the household of the faith" (Gal. 6:10). *Just as Paul had used the adverb "Above all else" in 1 Timothy 5:8 to prioritize responsibility of one's family over others, so he does now to prioritize responsibility of provision for those, "who are the household generated from the faith" over against "all men."*

The testimony of the Apostle John and James are in agreement: "But if anyone has the world's goods, and sees his brother in need, yet closes his heart against them, how does God's love abide in him?" (1 Jn. 3:17)

"If a brother or sister is ill-clad and in lack of daily food, and one of you says to them, 'Go in peace, be warmed and filled,' without giving them the things needed for the body, what does it profit?" (James 2:15–16).

The Christian citizen's next social responsibility, according to Scripture, is to the Body of Christ, before society in general. Jesus had stated, "By this all men will know that you are My disciples, if you have love for one another" (Jn. 13:35).

History bears out how often Christians shouldered this principle of social responsibility out toward one another. Tertullian wrote about the common Roman cultural statement concerning Christians, "Look, they say, 'how they love one another…and how they are ready to die for each other'"[18] For the Christian citizen of God's Kingdom, the priority of responsibility starts first with personal provision, then extends to his family's provision, and then extends further to the Body of Christ. *As far as the government is concerned, they are to be concerned about the priorities of yourself and your family. This third "Body of Christ" Biblical application does not directly concern the government.*

Fourth, Take Care of Your Neighbor 3

Returning to Galatians 6:10, the Apostle Paul stated, "So then, as we have opportunity, let us do good to all men." The pronoun *all* here is an inclusive pronoun meaning "all without distinction." Of course, as was pointed out earlier, the following adverb *especially* pointed to the priority of "doing good" to the household of the faith. We return now to the imperative of responsibility to "be working good to all without distinction," the final outer circle of responsibility but a great one at that. In 1 Timothy 6:18, we are given a general characterization by which Christians should be known: "Instruct them to do good, to be rich in good works, to be generous and ready to share."

The summation of the first priority of responsibility to the government lies in what God's will is for His Kingdom citizens. If a Christian is responsible to God's will to provide for ourselves, our families, the Body of Christ, and for others in general, he will have fulfilled the most basic of responsibilities for his earthly government. This same paradigm of responsibility is equally true to any US citizen (with the exception to their responsibility to provide for the Body of Christ, if they are not a Believer).

For this next responsibility, as my mama would say, "Hold on to your britches!" There is not only the responsibility of life and property provision but also to that of life and property protection. In order for you to fulfill your responsibility to God and government in <u>PROVISION</u>, you also have a responsibility of <u>PROTECTION</u> of the very same people involved!

We began with our responsibility to God to provide for self, family, and neighbors. Consequently, we observed this becomes our first responsibility to government as well. Now, within this section, we will look at the natural extension from that responsibility to our responsibility to God and government to protect one's life and property. Once again, however, we must begin with a Biblical foundation from which we can draw principles of life and property protection. The Scriptures will again inform our ethics and political disposition with government. The underlying question to be answered from the Biblical evidence is, "Do we have an obligation before God to resist evil and to protect life and property?" The natural application of the answer to that question will then define our responsibility to government! Yes, this where we understand the Biblical view of the use of weapons (read "guns," if you wish) for protection purposes.

Biblical Foundations Concerning Protection (A Short Bible Study Time That You May Not See in Most Churches)

Several building principles must be laid. I call them the "Sacred Life Triad." The first of these is: <u>Human life is precious because of the image of God within each human being; therefore, the only proper and equivalent punishment for murdering any human is to take the life of the murderer</u>. Genesis 9:6 states, "Whoever sheds man's blood, by man his blood shall be shed, for in the image of God He made man."

The basis for an individual's life value is rooted in the declaration by God, "for in the image of God He made man." Because of that intrinsic value within every human, regardless of race, age, in and out of the womb, or economic status, "murder was to be punished with death because it destroyed the image of God in man."[19] This passage lays the basis for capital punishment by the government and the premise for both self-defense and the defense of others.

What must not be missed is that subtle, underlying ethic of the basis for the defense of life. "As all the judicial relations and ordinances of the increasing race were rooted in those of the family, and grew by a natural process out of that, the family relations furnished of themselves the norm."[20] In other words, historically, governmental Justice grew from the family system and later into formalized government. Initially, it was the family's obligation to enact Justice and protection. Only later, as in this passage, was the baton passed onto a governmental obligation of capital punishment. What must be stressed is that in God's eyes, all human lives have equal value because of the *imago dei*, or to parody a current colloquial saying, "All lives matter!" To take a human life is punishable by the equivalent taking of the perpetrator's life. The obligation of the preservation of human life by preventing that crime simply is derived from that principle, as we shall now see in the following passages.

The second building principle of the "Sacred Life Triad" is <u>There is a Biblical obligation to proactively preserve life.</u> Ezekiel 33:6 states, "But if the watchman sees the sword coming and does not blow the trumpet, and the people are not warned, and the sword comes and takes a person from them…his blood I will require from the watchman's hand." Contextually, God is speaking to Ezekiel about his obligation as a prophet to warn the people of judgment. YHWH simply states a known dictum of Justice (the watchman's moral obligation) to make His point to Ezekiel about his prophetic obligation. *That dictum of Justice is "cast in the style of casuistic (conditional) law. Typically casuistic Law begins with a protasis…followed by an apodosis stating the legal consequence of the action described in the apodosis."[21] Stated simply, "If you do (or don't) do this, then consequently this will (or won't) happen to you." That dictum of Justice cannot be dismissed; "it is the duty of the appointed watchman of a land to announce to the people the approach of the enemy, and if he fail to do this he is deserving of death."[22]* As a watchman, it was his duty to warn of imminent danger, an obligation to preserve life and "his exhortation to individual responsibility."[23]

That responsibility to preserve other's lives is to be both proactive and preventative. Even the building "code" to be followed in early Israel was meant for a neighbor to protect others from death,

"When you build a new house, you shall make a parapet for your roof, that you may not bring bloodshed on your house if anyone falls from it" (Deut. 22:8). Keil and Delitzsch place this Law under the heading of "The duty to love one's neighbor." [24] The point God made to Israel was that they were to love their neighbor by protecting them from possible harm or death.

This collection of civil laws in Deuteronomy were laws set to regulate Justice and the "Community's relation to God." [25] Civil Law is a means by which an individual and community properly relate to God. Laws are not meant to be merely arbitrary. Laws are to be based upon the higher laws of God (c.f. chapter 1 for the development of this premise). Within the context of this discussion, civil Law is to proactively protect one's neighbor from harm, and that is to love that neighbor and to love God. It is a responsibility to love God and neighbor by protecting the lives within their home.

A similar statement of Justice and obligation is made in Psalm 82:3–4: "Vindicate the weak and fatherless; do Justice to the afflicted and destitute. Rescue the weak and needy; deliver them out of the hand of the wicked." *Again, the revered interpreters of Scripture, Keil and Delitzsch, state about this passage, "The right over life and death, with which the administration of Justice cannot dispense, is a prerogative of God. He has transferred the execution of this prerogative to mankind." To not do so, is to, "judge unjustly, לפט צול " [26] Again, the context is to those delegated in community to execute Justice (government). However, once again, the underlying premise is that life is to be proactively protected from harm. Any individual's intervention to prevent a capital crime from occurring is for that individual to "judge justly." The community government was to decide if that was so in that particular case.* The Wisdom literature gives the imperative, "Deliver those who are being taken away to death, and those who are staggering to slaughter, O hold them back" (Proverbs 24:11).

The third building principle from the "Sacred Life Triad" is Lethal force can be used in self (and neighbor) defense. Exodus 22:2–3 dictates, "If the thief is caught while breaking in, and is so struck so that he dies, there will be no blood-guiltiness on his account." Notice that it states that the perpetrator in question is a "thief," not a murderer or a rapist *per se.* It is a matter of self-defense, defense of family, and defense of property. The next verse presumes that if the same occurrence happens during the day, one cannot kill the thief but that the "thief" must be held at bay for apprehension to pay for his thievery (vv. 1, 4). At night, in the cover of darkness, intentions, identification, and inequality of means and ability are vague enough to warrant stopping the thief, even if it is by lethal force ("struck, so that he dies"). *Many commentators have discussed the ambiguity of the second half of this dictum. In the end, the general agreements is that the "thief" in the daylight scenario presumably no longer holds the "upper hand" of greater ability and force in the light of day as he had in the darkness.*

A passage in Nehemiah 4:8–23 displays a racial tension and opposition that warranted the people of God to arm themselves to protect life and property. The telling verse is Nehemiah's words of encouragement in verse 14: "Fight for your brothers, your sons, your daughters, your wives and your houses." This is not a wartime scenario in which people have been conscripted by the government to fight a war. These are civilians attempting to build their city and houses (property) amid racial threats. Under the threat of physical harm from Sanballat and Tobiah, these civilians "operated on the principle that God helps those who help themselves. They prayed to God with their lips while they defended themselves physically by posting guards." The purpose was to "protect the structure and the builders."[27]

Two outstanding ethical points can be drawn from this text. One, defense by lethal means (the sword is an "assault weapon") was not just pertaining to life or physical harm but also of property. Two, there is no conflict between praying and trusting God, while at the same time carrying a weapon. A contemporary saying that illustrates this Biblical idea is, "When on your knees, pray as if everything depends upon God, and it does. When you get up off of your knees, work as if everything depends upon you, and it does."

Now I begin some more fighting words! Let's turn to a New Testament passage to see if our conclusions thus far are in harmony with Jesus's words. Luke 22:35–39 will be the focus passage. We had concluded in chapter 1 that Jesus introduced a paradigm shift in which it is made clear that the Gospel insurgence is not to be by the sword. However, and carefully note this, He then introduces a shift to personal self-defense by means of the sword with these abrupt and thought transitioning words "But now" (Αλλα νυν).

Please indulge me another moment with some Greek text analysis for any doubtful Biblical scholar. The periphrastic "ο μη εκων...μακαιραν" enveloping the aorist imperative "he is to buy" (αγορασατο) should not be missed for the forceful and striking tone from Jesus that it is. There is urgency in His command to buy a lethal weapon. Furthermore, the word used for "sword" is an idiom for "war" (Matt. 10:34), or "violent death" (Rom 8:35). Geisler concludes from Jesus' Gospel narratives about swords,

> That is, swords are not valid weapons to fight spiritual battles, but they are legitimate tools for one's civil defense. Herein seems to be the sanction of Jesus to the justifiable use of an instrument of death in defense against an unjust aggressor. That is, Jesus commanded the use of the sword as a means of civil defense.[28]

When the disciples replied to Jesus's command about purchasing swords, they did so with these responsive words: "Look, Lord, here are two swords." He then said, "It is enough (Ικανον εστιν)" (v. 38). "Ικανον" has the connotation of "worthy," or even "security" or "peace bond."[29] The idea is, "two swords are good enough for security."

Therefore, together we conclude that one, Jesus warranted the use of deadly weapons, not for the promotion of the Gospel but for civil defense. Two, Jesus expected His disciples to be armed, and He commanded them to purchase a sword, even more urgently than the purchasing of garments. Carl F. H. Henry, in a lengthy discussion of the Sermon on the Mount, makes it quite clear that the Sermon is based upon the Old Testament and that it does not deny defense by force: "God punishes Israel for idolatry, for adultery, for disregard of the Sabbath, but not for resort to war in self-defense. In fact, he often commands their participation in such a war."[30] In his comments, Dr.

Henry was making application to a national defense ethic. However, we seek only to prove that the idea of a New Testament God being against lethal force to preserve life is shown to be false.

Although we have not exhausted all the Scriptures on this particular ethic, the inescapable conclusion from the Scriptures is that we all have, as human beings, as citizens and as God's people, an obligation before God to resist evil and protect life, and sometimes even property. The Scriptures may or may not be explicit about self-defense and defense of others because frankly, it is an underlying assumption that bleeds into other explicit passages. For you, the citizen, that obligation is before God first, and therefore, that same obligation then becomes your responsibility to our government. If God expects people to defend life and property, our government should expect no less from her citizens, particularly from those who honor God.

Notice how much debate, media coverage, and passionate, ill-informed opinions come from a section of government and culture against this sacred Biblical premise. Why is that? I say, it is because the opposition to this Biblical responsibility is to put certain privileged humans in charge in the place of God and His Justice.

The approach of this study began with the aspect that God's people, equipped with this knowledge, were to instruct government and educate our culture on what the citizen responsibilities were to their government. Those responsibilities are dictated by God, not the government, except in those cases where the government's Law is in alignment with God's Law. No political platform can override the heart and will of God on the matter! Using the Great Commandment as a guide once again as we did in the previous section on the provision of life and property, we will now make direct application for the protection of life and property.

Your Second Responsibility to Government: Life and Property Protection

So are you shocked yet? Are you now fighting mad? Righteously so! You have learned from the Biblical truth of Scripture that there are three foundational principles, the "Sacred Life Triad," laid out in the above section. First: human life is precious because of the *imago dei* within them; therefore, the only proper and equivalent punishment for murdering any human is to take the life of the murderer (and as a side note, the "death penalty" is God's idea). Second: we have a Biblical obligation to proactively preserve life. Third: we can use lethal force in defense of self (and neighbor). This "Sacred Life Triad" is the basis for which we are to inform our governments of our responsibility to them, and to educate friends, family, educators, and any dissenters as well.

We must make a critical distinction before we proceed any further. There is an ethical and moral distinction between two important terms. "It may be helpful to distinguish between 'force' and 'violence.' While all violence is force, not all force is violence. Appropriate force is motivated by Justice and love…it is aimed at restoring peace. Violence is not inspired by Justice and love but by greed and hatred; it is not aimed at restoring peace but at destruction and evoking terror."[31] In short, we do not believe in the use of violence. We believe in the use of force to stop violence. When someone starts swinging a baseball bat to attack/rob/rape you, they are using "violence." When you pull a gun and fire on them to stop them, you are using "force," or "justifiable force."

As we pursue the subject of self-defense, we are using the word *force* in its ethical meaning as a godly means to defend life, as opposed to *violence*. Also, as mentioned earlier, godly self-defense is always to be about seeking Justice, not revenge. Defense of life is about "Justice in the moment" when needed. Retaliation and revenge is one seeking to be judge, jury and executioner, which is the State's God-given role.

Self-Protection

Within the Great Commandment, we saw that love of God came first, and within that context, we are to love ourselves. As we look into the use of force, I had previously dealt with my foundations on the issue of pacifism within the introduction. At times, I will repeat the Biblical rationale from that section to speak of our responsibility to government to protect our personal lives, and that of our neighbor's as well.

I now repeat a critical and essential Biblical teaching for serious thought. One should not easily dismiss the statement that Jesus made in Luke 22:36. He introduces a paradigm shift from the Gospel promulgation which is not by the sword, to personal self-defense by the sword with these striking words: "But now" (Αλλα νυν). The periphrastic "ο μη εκων...μακαιραν" enveloping the aorist imperative "he is to buy" (αγορασατο) should not be missed for the forceful tone from Jesus that it is. Furthermore, the word used for sword is an idiom for "war" (Matt. 10:34) or "violent death" (Rom 8:35). Geisler concludes from Jesus' Gospel narratives about swords, "That is, swords are not valid weapons to fight spiritual battles, but they are legitimate tools for one's civil defense. Herein seems to be the sanction of Jesus to the justifiable use of an instrument of death in defense against an unjust aggressor. That is, Jesus commanded the use of the sword as a means of civil defense."[32] Jesus was not without the practice of the use of force against evil when He cleansed the Temple on at least one occasion (Mark 11 and John 2). The "whip" was also a weapon of force in His day, and His zealous use of it "looks like a clear use of force and the resisting of evildoers."[33]

The compelling argument is that the use of force (not violence) by the Christian in opposing evil perpetrators is not simply limited to a couple of passages. A larger, systematic Biblical picture must be used to base one's conviction on these views rather than mere "verse picking" to prove one's point. When someone finds themselves placing verses into adversarial positions against each other, we are at fault, not God's revelation. I believe this is the weakness to the pacifist viewpoint, as Copan and Flannigan stated, "To impose a nonviolent or pacifistic grid on the words and actions of God/Jesus requires significant hermeneutical gymnastics—an approach that creates an interpretive straitjacket." [34]

A passage used frequently to object to self-defense is Jesus's statement in the Sermon, "whoever slaps you on your right cheek, turn to him the other also" (Matt.5:39). This statement by our King is surgically excised from its historical context. This is a statement about personal insult, not of physical harm to one's self. The right cheek being struck necessitates a backhanded strike, "according to Rabbinical Law to hit a man with the *back* of the hand was twice as insulting as to hit him with the *flat* of the hand." [35]

Alexander Bruce, professor of Apologetics in Glasgow explains, "The right cheek is only named first according to common custom, (*and* is) not supposed to be struck first"[36] (clarifying italics mine). In other words, Jesus's call is to humbly stand one's ground amidst escalating personal insults. This passage has nothing to do with "use of force" to protect life; it is a prohibition against returning insult for insult. One cannot hold to a pacifist Jesus or a prohibition of His followers from ever using force without ignoring the momentous evidence of the rest of Scripture. Paul, Stephen, John, and the author of Hebrews all preach a God who has, does, and will act with gruesome force, "the grid of pacifism/nonviolence seems to go against other affirmations in the New Testament." [37]

The New Testament does not promote a pacifist disposition on God's part nor toward His people, and therefore not upon citizens. It also teaches forgiveness and the breaking of evil in society[38] and to have a "sacrificial, loving response to maintain a non-vindictive, magnanimous, reconciling attitude in all personal relationships when one's own rights or honor are at stake," while expecting government to do its job of Justice.[39] Listen to this truth carefully: simultaneous with the time-honored ethic of loving and forgiving our enemy, we are not prevented from using force to prevent and stop their evil actions.

One's life is sacred before God, as are all human beings made in God's image. If we are to love ourselves as God loves us, we will protect and defend our life. This disposition of treating everyone's life as sacred, including our own, is to have a Doppler effect in our society. "In this and in many other ways, the moral standards demanded of the citizen of God inevitably affect the moral standards of the Kingdoms of men." [40] As argued in chapter 1, it does no good to split these two, salvation of men and redemption of culture, into two camps as God Himself does not. To do so would be just as erroneous as to separate "make disciples of all men" (Matt. 25:19) from

"Let your light shine before all men" (Matt.5:16). We are to protect our own lives as a responsibility before God, and therefore, we are to protect our own lives as a responsibility to our government. Government is to expect us to protect ourselves; it is not primarily their responsibility!

The natural effect of the citizen doing so will have a positive effect upon society around us: "salt" and "light." This responsibility includes the use of deadly force, if necessary. The protection of property, which sustains our life, is a necessary appendage to that ethic. Our government is to expect the citizens to protect themselves. This point is reflected in the legal doctrine of the United States. Repeatedly, courts have held that the government has no responsibility to provide individual security. One particular case put it this way: "there is no constitutional right to be protected by the state against being murdered."[41] On the legal books of case Law at least, jurisprudence is in agreement with the Biblical self-defense ethic.

The statistics of following that righteous truth prove themselves out. "Guns prevent an estimated 2.5 million crimes a year or 6,849 every day. This includes rapes, aggravated assaults, and kidnappings. Often the gun is never fired and no blood (including the criminal's) is shed." [42] If a government seeks the good of its citizens (c. f. chapter 1), then it will want citizens to protect their own lives. Those on the front lines of Law enforcement largely agree, "66% of police chiefs agree that citizens carrying concealed firearms reduce rates of violent crimes."[43] Interestingly, criminals agree to this righteous ethic by default, and thereby show the "salt" and "light" impact of the armed citizen's love for God, self, and neighbor: "74% of felons agree that, 'one reason burglars avoid houses when people are at home is that they fear being shot during the crime' and 57% of felons polled agreed, 'criminals are more worried of meeting an armed victim than they are about running into the police."[44] Furthermore, "60% of convicted felons admitted that they avoided committing crimes when they <u>knew</u> the victim was armed. 40% of convicted felons admitted that they avoided committing crimes when they <u>thought</u> the victim might be armed."[45]

These statistics are not the basis from which to form a Biblical viewpoint on the use of force to protect ourselves. However, they do reflect the realistic effectiveness of a Biblical ethic of self-defense.

Protection of your Neighbor

We observed from the exposition of Scripture earlier that the responsibility to <u>provide</u> for one self and for their neighbor was based upon the Great Commandment. We have now observed that the <u>protection</u> of oneself and property is based upon that same commandment. It is an easy transition to then understand that the protection of one's neighbor (the first of which is family) is an extension of loving God, and therefore a responsibility to our government.

The responsibility to protect other lives begins with the family. Again, to quote Paul, "If any one does not provide for his own, and especially those of his own household, he has denied the faith and is worse than an unbeliever" (1 Tim. 5:8). *Paul prioritizes one's own family above others with the Greek adverb, "μαλιστα," meaning "above all else."* Our first "neighbor" to protect is our spouse, our children, and our extended family, and in that order. *Of course, the citizen is not to try to protect everybody, as that is not even possible. There is a hierarchy to social ethics. It begins with our family, followed by our neighbor. "And who is my neighbor?" is a valid question from a lawyer (Luke 10:29). Dr. Norman Geisler states that Jesus's parable of the Good Samaritan shows that the Samaritan was neighborly to the victim of crime and we are to "love any fellow human being in need" within our closest proximal or circumstantial context, and that "the best way to do that is to love one's immediate family and friends as best we can."* [46]

In practical, ethical, and legal terms, we are not to appoint ourselves as a vigilante group of one, nor of many. That is the government's God-appointed role. But do not miss this crucial point: we are to practice "Justice in the moment" to protect our self, our family, and any other human being in the immediate need of defense. Nehemiah's call to "fight for your families, your sons and daughters, your wives and your homes" (Neh. 4:14) was a collective call to a family community under attack in a non-war situation. They were to defend themselves, their families, their property, and, collectively, their neighbors as well. In fact, like the watchman in Ezekiel who did not act proactively to protect people under imminent attack, we become an accomplice to the crime before God.

Therefore, a citizen has a responsibility to God and government to protect not only themselves but also others who are in our proximity at the time of danger. In fact, there are laws in some states that will prosecute a bystander to a crime if they did not act in a judicious manner at the time. "God commanded love for one's neighbor (Lev. 19:18), but this love was not in opposition to capital punishment in the Law of Moses."[47] By the same rule of logic and Biblical ethics, one must love their neighbor by protecting them, even if by lethal force, if necessary.

God gave us the Great Commandment as a template for life in which we are to love God first, ourselves second within that love relationship with God, and our neighbor third. In application to our responsibilities to our government, we are to live a righteous, ethical lifestyle, which includes the proper provision of physical needs for our self, our family, and our neighbor. That physical need provision for all persons concerned may necessitate their protection and preservation from physical harm as well as the preservation of property. Lethal force, if necessary, may be used. The government should expect no less and no more from her citizens.

When Government Disagrees with Your Godly Responsibilities

Your primary allegiance is to the King and His Kingdom. If we are committed, faithful followers of God and His Kingdom, we may well observe the two Kingdoms coming into conflict with each other. There can and even should be tensions between these Kingdoms at times. There may be a haunting question that lies behind our position of instructing government concerning our God-dictated responsibilities to them: "But, but, but, what if the government doesn't take well to that Godly perspective or, what if our government completely ignores our convictions?"

The King Takes king

Do you fight, or do you roll over and play dead? Like the elephant in the room that everyone awkwardly evades, the daunting dilemma is what Charles Colson called "Kingdoms in Conflict." The reason there are Kingdoms in conflict is that there is a Primal King over all governments. In his book by that very name, Colson asserts, "The conflict is particularly apparent in the Judeo-Christian tradition because the assertion that the God of both the Old and New Testament Scriptures is King. That has been an offense to the proud and powerful from the beginning-and the reason Jews and Christians alike have been systematically persecuted."[48]

Whether it is the king of a monarchy, a president of the United States or a Supreme Court judge, governmental leaders do not like being reminded of that small voice in their conscience of their accountability to the Great Lawgiver, the Primal King. *This is because Christianity's "transcendent vision holds the world accountable to something beyond itself" and her "members serve as ambassadors, citizens of the heavenly Kingdom at work in this world."* [49] The Christian citizen is to be a pesky voice of conscience to the government. *Government would rather operate, as Nietzsche described it, as if "God is dead." "God is dead, not because He doesn't exist, but because we live, play, procreate, govern and die as though He doesn't."* [50]

Dietrich Bonhoeffer goes so far as to say, "Jesus Christ possesses all power in heaven and on earth (Matt. 28:18), and He is, therefore, also the Lord of government. Its goal is Jesus Christ Himself. Its purpose is to serve Him." [51] As the Creator of the universe (Col. 1:16), as the Head of all authority in heaven and on earth (Matt. 28:18), Jesus Christ is King of the universe, whether individuals or governments know it or not, or whether they accept it or not. What defines the Christian citizen is that we have submitted to that Kingship as His children and as His eternal citizens living in this temporal, worldly Kingdom of men. We live as citizens of both, with primary allegiance to the eternal King first. When those kings come in conflict, His crown rules first. *A lengthier discourse on this doctrine is delineated in the Introduction.*

The King Takes queen

What is the Christian citizen's primary Kingdom? Since we have a First King, we also have a First Kingdom. Using the above chess game analogy, the King takes the little king's queen, his Kingdom. The Church is not "the" Kingdom of God, but is a part of God's Kingdom, and she acts as His Kingdom ambassadors. Christianity bears the responsibility to be the torchbearers of their King-Leader's purpose here on earth: "For this I have been born, and for this I have come into the world, to bear witness to the truth" (John 18:37*).* *The aorist subjunctive, "μαρτυπησω," "bear witness," preceded by the purpose particle, "ινα," "in order to" and in the relationship to the two perfect verbs, "γεγεννημαι," "I have been born" and "εληλυθα," "I have come" are inspirationally instructive. The divinely inspired grammatical syntax reveals the following reality: Long before His conception within Mary on this world, the Eternal Counsel purposed to send the Second Person of the Godhead onto earth for a very clear objective: to testify to the truth. What is meant by, "αληθειασ," "truth" here? Francis Schaeffer gives us the depiction of this word's etymology:*

> *When I say Christianity is true I mean it is true to total reality-the total of what is, beginning with the central reality, the objective existence of the person-al-infinite God. Christianity is not just a series of truths but Truth-Truth about all of reality. And the holding to that truth intellectually—and in some poor way living upon that Truth, the Truth of what is-brings forth not only certain personal results, but also governmental and legal results.[52]*

Those last words portray real world results; if we are bearers of His Truth, it will influence Law and governments! "What is it about the Judeo-Christian message that makes it so offensive?…the heart of the Gospel-that Christ is King." Colson says from his world travel experience that the enemies of God's Kingdom understand this "better than many in the 'Christian' West." [53] Therefore, the burden of the Christian citizen is to "bear witness to the truth" as your King did and does through you. The impact has a twofold perspective, the eternal one—"My Kingdom does not originate from this world" (John 18:36, my translation)—and the temporary one of "salt and light," which gives "governmental and legal results." Historically, this is not a foreign concept to Christianity. It is only because in the last few decades within our Country we have been blinded by our culture and deluded by irresponsible theology from our pulpits that all this seems strange.

Two Halves of Your Responsibility to God's Kingdom

I personally do not come from the tradition of the "whole Gospel" movement. I will, however, let you know that Christianity here in the Western Church has split God's work and reality in and through us into two halves, a "spiritual-eternal and heavenly, 'I'll fly away'" half and the, "physical, earthly, God doesn't really care about it" half. That thinking comes as an infection from the Greek Gnosticism philosophy, and not from God's Word and heart!

The First Half You May Not Be Missing:
The Eternal Perspective

Since the focus of this book's thesis is concerning the relationship of citizens and their government, little will be addressed as to the eternal perspective of God's Kingdom. Instead, the concentration will be upon the earthly yet highly significant, cultural mandate. However, the following acknowledges the eternal perspective of God's Kingdom.

In Matthew 28:18, the resurrected Jesus stated, "All authority is given me without exception, in heaven and upon this earth. Therefore, you all make disciples without distinction of all the nations while you are going about; by baptizing them into the name of the Father, and of the Son, and of the Holy Spirit and by teaching them how to keep all things I commanded you. Furthermore, look, I myself am with you all of these earthly days, even to the consummation of the ages" (my translation).

Based upon this designation of all-encompassing Kingship by the Godhead to Jesus Christ, Jesus then outlines a lifestyle mission to make a difference for eternity. This "eternal mandate" to make disciples of Jews and Gentiles without distinction is found throughout the New Testament *(which truly began in full at His crucifixion, resurrection, and ascension, not at the beginning of the Gospels).* The people of God through faith in Jesus Christ the Savior and King are charged to make disciples of others as His sovereignty works through them, by His Spirit, to bring about spiritual life. This lifestyle mission brings about newly birthed disciples and matures them as effective disciple makers.

Other than the work of sanctification in which one seeks to be a better disciple, the coup de grace of the Christian life is to be evangelizing and discipling others in the Christian faith. Thus, one is making an eternal difference in the lives of others and is paying allegiance to God's Kingdom through the eternal perspective. This perspective is indeed critical and worthy of our King. This eternal mandate we as Christian citizens are quite familiar with, even if not very effective at it. However, this mandate is only half of the command of Christ, the other half of which has been largely ignored. Not only is there the eternal perspective of God's Kingdom and its mandate, there is also the temporal perspective and its mandate.

The Second Half You Are Probably Missing: Change the World Now (The "Cultural Mandate")

It was John Wesley who said, "There is no holiness but social holiness" and to make it "into a solitary religion is to destroy it."[54] Wesley was simply saying that your faith in God, in Christ, is meaningless if you are not permeating your family, society, and culture (and government). Jesus not only commanded, "You all make disciples" (the only command in the "Great Commission"), but He also states, "You are the salt of the earth... You are the light of the world..."

(Matt. 5:13–14). Jesus describes His disciples in their God-given state of being *the existential essence of who they are to be ("υμεισ εστε… ")*. He then goes on to warn them of their impotence as His disciples if they are not being so. This is known as the "Cultural Mandate" of the Church, as Francis Schaeffer reminds us:

> The old revivals are spoken about so warmly by the evangelical leadership. Yet they seem to have forgotten what those revivals were. Yes, the old revivals…did call, without any question… for personal salvation. But they also called for a resulting social action. Yet even secular historians acknowledge that it was the social results coming out of the Wesley revival that saved England from its own form of the French Revolution.[55]

Schaeffer goes on to give examples of William Wilberforce's impact to end slavery and of Lord Shaftesbury standing for the poor in the midst of the Industrial Revolution. In his chapter entitled "Plan for Action," Constitutional attorney John Whitehead emphatically states, "The Church has a mandate from the Creator to be a dominant influence on the whole culture." He adds that we start now "by putting God and the Bible first and recognizing that Christ is Lord over all areas of life. Then we are ready for action."[56] The mandate for the Church—or in our context, you, the Christian citizen—is to be just as passionate about Christ's kingship influencing this world's culture as you are with the eternal mandate. In answer to naysayers to this Cultural Mandate, none other than the respected, world-renowned theologian Dr. Carl F. H. Henry asks,

> Does the New Testament ethic really disclose no positive concern whatever for the earth-world, and does it rule out all consideration of earthly interests and values? Both Jesus and Paul share the belief that the Kingdom of God has already impinged upon history in a supreme and decisive

> way through the incarnation…and both look to
> a future superlative climax applying the conse-
> quences to the whole human race.[57]

What Dr. Henry addresses here has been reduced to a common saying among theologians in speaking about: "God's Kingdom is already, but not yet." Christ's Kingdom is moving toward an ultima, a crescendo of climactic history, and He has invited you to be history-makers with Him! This is the, "Blessed Hope" we all share as His people.

In the meantime, however, the movement of Christ's Kingdom is to be penetrating the present world through us, His Kingdom citizens. *An eschatological point of distinction should be made here. None of the theologians I have referenced here is speaking of the Cultural Mandate as a "Postmillennial" doctrine. In fact, neither myself, nor any of the theologians referenced, are postmillennialists looking to bring about a utopian "millennium" through the Church.* The Cultural Mandate is simply a doctrine of obedience to Christ to shape both time with eternity for His Name's sake, however imperfectly, this side of His Return. He promises His Presence as we do, and we have a catalog of heroes throughout history to prove it so! Will you join those heroes as well?

What Has Caused the Western Church to "Roll Over and Play Dead"?

Despite these clear teachings from Jesus and the Apostles on the "Cultural Mandate," the Church seems to have lost her way in this area. *"What sometimes escapes Christians is the fact that the responsibility to love other persons extends to the whole person. That is, man is more than a soul destined for another world; he is also a body living in this world. Some of the neglect for the "whole man" stems from a non-Christian platonic stress of the duality of man."*

In other words, the Church has generally adapted a heresy stemming from Greek philosophy that has practically discounted the present world almost entirely and has elevated "spiritual" concerns as superlative to all others. "As we turn to the evangelical leadership of this country in the last decades, unhappily, we must come to the conclusion that often it has not been much help. It has shown the mark of a platonic, overly spiritualized Christianity all too often. Spirituality…often has not included the Lordship of Christ over the whole spectrum of life."[58]

Schaeffer calls this a "defective view of Christianity," and what followed from it was a "Pietism (that) made a sharp division between the 'spiritual' and the 'material' world—giving little, or no, importance to the 'material' world."[59] In his analysis of the loss of the Cultural Mandate as part of the Gospel, Colson laments, "Christian values are in retreat in the West today, primarily, I believe, because of the Church itself. If Christianity has failed to stem the rising tides of relativism it is because the Church in many instances has lost the convicting force of the gospel message."[60]

Did you catch that phrase, "convicting force"? Do you think your government sees you, sees the Church as a "convicting force"? In what I detect as a righteous angry tone, Colson seems to scold Western Christians, "His followers have watered down His teaching, stripped away His demands for the building of a righteous society," and instead, "portrays Christianity not as the powerful source of spiritual rebirth and the mediating force for Justice, mercy, and love in the world, but as the ultimate self-fulfillment plan." [61] A contemporary Church planter echoes this Christian retreat from its responsibility,

> Under the good intentions of well-meaning leaders, the Church has fallen back on her heels in a defensive posture, seeking refuge in its own fortresses of buildings, programs, and 'Christian' businesses, schools and ministries. Trying to avoid the threat we were always meant to thwart, we have lost ground over and over again until at last we have nowhere left to go, surrounded by wickedness. We are now seen as an impotent and frightened group that hides from the world and the reality that faces us. We have allowed

the enemy to take over the culture and society,
and we complain from the safety of our so-called
Christian strongholds.[62]

Our musical worship in Churches betray this "self-fulfillment plan" when the lyrics continually point to the singular worshipper. If one listens to their Church's typical music, it is rampant with self-focus ("He loves me, yeah, yeah, yeah") instead of singing as a corporate Body of Christ singing <u>to</u> their King.

Furthermore, the music has withdrawn from its offensive posture betrayed by its withdrawal from society. For example, when was the last time the hymn "We'll Work till Jesus Comes" or "Rise Up, O Men of God," or "Onward, Christian Soldiers" was heard, even in a contemporary style, in today's Church? We have been deluded into a "love-fest" concert instead of seeing ourselves as an army of soldiers.

A required textbook I had during my graduate studies claimed "Christians living in an increasingly pluralistic world, face an enlarging dilemma. Christians must come to grips with God's mandate that his people actively and aggressively share his message with all people…and seek their conversion."[63] What is plainly seen within this textbook is an impassioned call for the Church to rise up and be diligent about only half of the mandate, the eternal one.

There should be unanimous applause to this cry. However, the silence to the temporal, cultural mandate is altogether deafening. This is but a small sample of the theological "defect," as Francis Schaeffer called it, within the Church's theology, particularly in those of us in evangelical circles.

Have We Always Been This Wimpy?

This anemic and effeminate view of Christianity was not how Colonial America and the United States began. As noted earlier in the introduction, the Biblical map and compass of the land gave a formidable platform of Christianity, transforming society, law, and government. "A dominant aspect of the Christian influence on early nineteenth century America was the interest and energy it displayed toward the external world and society. This was the result of the application of the cultural mandate."[64] Even earlier, the Constitutional framers fought over not the separation of Christianity from the government; instead, they passionately fought against any governmental-Christian denomination over another.

Isaac Backus, Baptist clergyman and historian, and a Mayflower descendant,

> *In his lengthy tract, 'An appeal to the Public for Religious Liberty,' contains a strong, rhetorical Revolutionary-era argument for faith-based liberty. Illustrating his presentation with Biblical injunctions Backus went so far as to suggest that America could never become in spirit a true Christian nation until complete Church-state separation had been secured."* [65]

Put plainly, the First Amendment discussions were not about the influence of Christianity in government but of preventing government's interference into Church matters. *In an ironic note, when Massachusetts was settled in America by England, "King James II temporarily revoked Massachusetts's royal charter, due to restrictions the Puritans had imposed on their fellow Protestants limiting religious freedom and the right to worship."[66] For whatever motive, even the King of England, whom the Colonies would eventually revolt from, would personally be an arbitrator for religious freedom separate from state imposition and control.*

This research simply points to the Cultural Mandate given the Church by our King Jesus to impact culture righteously, as well as in all her laws and government. The two are destined, this side of heaven, to always be clumsy partners in an awkward dance. But dance we must; sitting on the sidelines we must not! The history of the Colonies, and later of the United States, in her founding documents, reveal this awkward dance on the dancing floor of politics.

Christianity and politics are not diametrically opposed to each other unless the State crosses certain lines. In which case, the government should be steeling themselves for the irritating blast of "salt and light" in their eyes.

How Do We Relate This Cultural Mandate to Our Government?

Dietrich Bonhoeffer claims, "The Church has the task of summoning the whole world to submit to the dominion of Jesus Christ. She testifies before government to their common Master." [67] Citizens of His Kingdom (don't forget, that's you) are in an instructional disposition toward government in these areas on behalf of our King, and not *vice-versa*. Just as we are to be independently self-provisional and self-protective, so are we to be in our transformation of society, individually even if no one else does, but optimally as a unified force with other citizens. We have a King who has commanded us to do so; no lesser king or government need try to restrain us. If they try to do so, history proves it will only exacerbate their troubles and prove to be an encouragement to the force of the Church ("The blood of the martyrs is the seed of the Church." concept). "Christians do not rely on government, but on their own penetration of society as 'salt and light'. This too is in obedience to a command of God that orders them to be the 'salt of the earth' and 'the light of the world'-the great cultural commission of the Kingdom."[68]

I Pledge Allegiance to My King, and to the Other King Too

You now know that there is a God-given, natural dual citizenship for the Christian citizen, the primary one being to the King and His Kingdom relevant to this earth and the secondary one to one's own indigenous, earthly government.

Arguably, this same dual citizenship is applicable generically to anyone who believes in the creator God of the universe who is the great moral Judge of all creation. (Thus the phrase, "Nature and Nature's God" in the Declaration of Independence. The terminology would heartily encompass both the Judeo-Christian map as well as the influence of the "Enlightenment," as investigated in the Introduction. However, the focus of this study is upon the Christian viewpoint.)

Although I am emphasizing the priority of the citizenship and loyalty to God's Kingdom, we are not to forget that we are to be "good" citizens, as God defines it, to our earthly government. I have previously emphasized this moral citizenship and loyalty to our government. We are to lead lives of proper relationship toward family, neighbors, and all others, including government, because, "love does no wrong to a neighbor; love therefore is the fulfillment of law" *("governmental law" in this context as an anarthrous construction, "νομου," refers to Paul's contextual admonition to good citizenship).*

The dual-citizenship tension came to a head early in Christianity during the time of Constantine. "Christians under Constantine began to wrestle with what it meant to have 'dual citizenship' in a heavenly Kingdom and an earthly one. This was a very new experiment. Paganism was waning, and Christians were trying to fill the vacuum and figure out how to run things."[69] John Calvin, however imperfectly, tried to bring a balance to this tension during the Reformation period. He called it the, "duplex in homine regimen" in which he sought a distinction of the "'spiritual' and 'temporal' jurisdiction" with the former informing the latter.[70] More recently, Dietrich Bonhoeffer called out this dual citizenship controversy with a clear definition from his own culture in Germany: "A clear distinction must be drawn between the secular and the spiritual authority, but the Christians are, nevertheless, at the same time citizens, and the citizens, whether they be believers or not, are at the same time subject to the claim of Jesus Christ."[71]

Historically, government does not want the influence of Christ's Kingdom into their affairs. Lord Melbourne, in his opposition to the abolition of slave trade, is famous for his saying, "Things have come to a pretty pass when religion is allowed to invade public life."[72] Those of us in the United States have forgotten that it was the Christian force of being salt and light that brought the end of slavery both in England and in the States. It was, however, Christians exercising their dual citizenship that brought about the demise of slavery. The price paid by earlier Christians to be salt and light in our culture and to government has been practically dismissed. "We have forgotten why we have a high view of life, and why we have a positive balance between form and freedom in government. They are unique based on the fact that the consensus was the Biblical consensus." [73]

Constantine, Calvin, Bonhoeffer, and a plethora of theologians during and between those periods, and even up to this day, may argue the finer points of how the two kingships may relate to one another. However, there is a universal consensus that within this dual citizenship, the supremacy of Christ's kingship is unquestionable. A prophet of our time heralded the choice: "It is not too strong to say that we are at war, and there are no neutral parties in the struggle. One either confesses that God is the final authority, or one confesses that Caesar is Lord." [74] Since indeed to the resurrected Jesus "all authority is given in heaven and upon the earth," under His marching orders, we are to, "make disciples."

To echo Bonhoeffer's statement, we are to bring His Kingship to all, even to "the citizens, whether they be believers or not, (who) are at the same time subject to the claim of Jesus Christ." This responsibility extends to the culture around us, and even to our governmental authorities who are subject to their King, "whether they be believers or not." Indeed, the Christian citizen has a responsibility to the State as clarified earlier. However, "one should always obey government when it takes its rightful place *under* God, but one should never obey government when it takes the place *of* God."[75]

As discussed earlier, the goal of the citizens experiencing dual citizenship is not to bring about a "Christian theocracy," as some allege. Each sphere of government and Church are unique to themselves, yet they are both God's created institutions. It is the duty of the one sphere to inform, to influence, and to modify, if needed, the institution of government. From a historical point of view, "the record of the centuries should not cause despair, however. Tension between Church and state is inherent and inevitable. Indeed, it is perhaps the outworking of one of God's great mysteries, part of the dynamic by which He governs His universe. For from the constant tension-the chafing back and forth—certain equilibrium is achieved."[76]

Colson goes on to rightly state what I have previously referred to in this Church-state tension as "the Awkward Dance." The Church, as part of God's Kingdom, does not seek to overpower and to rule government but to be its nagging conscience, to be salt and light to government. *The background struggles to produce the First Amendment to the Constitution of the United States are seen in that "Thomas Jefferson would soon stress the importance of freedom from religion to avoid coercion; in the original Baptist spirit (Isaac) Backus placed his emphasis on freedom for religion."*[77]

On the one hand, the Founding Fathers had experienced governmental Church impositions within the Colonies' freedoms. This is what Jefferson feared. On the other hand, the same Fathers and the Colonies had experienced governmental intrusions upon the freedom of their Churches. This is what Isaac Backus feared and fought against. In the end, the First Amendment protected against what Jefferson feared: "Congress shall make no Law respecting an establishment of religion" and freed Churches from governmental intrusions upon their faith, or prohibiting the free exercise thereof." Within the First Amendment, the Church has no limitations upon influencing the government. However, that same amendment prohibits government from attempting to influence the Church. How well is our Country doing on that right now?

Charles Colson gave further illumination to the point of prioritization from the Scriptures: "But when Christ commanded His followers to 'seek first the Kingdom of God' He was exhorting them to seek to be ruled by God and gratefully acknowledge His power and authority over them. That means that the Christian's goal is not to strive to rule, but *to be ruled.*"[78] The Biblical data seems to support Colson's point here, and I couldn't agree more wholeheartedly. When Jesus said, "You all keep seeking *(ζητειτε—keep being on the watch for, keep endeavoring for')* God's Kingdom and His Righteousness," He wasn't on an attack against materialism, as some suppose. Rather, in context, Jesus was addressing the correct prioritization of His Kingdom world over our temporal world *("And all these things shall be added to you, ταυτα παντα προστεθησεται υμιν")*. The present impera-

tive to "keep seeking" is followed by a future, passive verb "shall proceed." It is a simple command to prioritize God's Kingdom and His rightful relationships with a promise, "The rest will take care of itself."

The temporal world, along with society and government in our context, takes secondary place to the King's rulership over us. Nevertheless, when Christ commanded us to seek first His Kingdom, that mandate immediately puts His disciples into a relationship with earthly Kingdoms that may at times be seen as antagonistic by the government. Indeed, seeking God's Righteousness to influence government may cause conflict, and that conflict may be a resistance against government by differing degrees of force.

No More Talk, It's Time to Fight!

The reality is that in most countries, and even in the United States, government officials and institutions are not comprised of believers in Christ in the eternal sense, much less submissive to his Kingship in the temporal sense, or even recognize "nature and nature's God" in the Judeo-Christian sense as in our Constitution. This is not to dismiss the fact that there are men and women of moral character within government. God indeed is a realist as He created reality *(John 14:6, "I am the truth, αληθεια, the word for "reality")*, and seemingly planned for the two distinct spheres when He created the two Kingdoms. With this reality comes the conflict between the Kingdoms, as well as the conflict between those of dual citizenships. We will now turn to the responsibility the Christian citizen, the Church, and anyone else with a moral compass has to resist government. From the accumulative argument from the Scriptures and history, I will argue for three levels of ascending force necessary to change society and government as God intended.

Fighting-Stage 1: Aggressive Political Action

The first stage of resistance to wrong or evil within our society and government is aggressive political action. For too long, a false dichotomy has separated Christianity from politics and political action.

Throughout this journey, we have asserted the following Biblical argument: It is God's will that His Kingdom citizens are to be His agents in society and government. The word politics *comes from the Greek word* politicos, *meaning, "of, or relating to citizens." Citizens are people, and God created people in His image.*

The Church has a responsibility under God to be a transformational force in the affairs of citizens on every level. "The real issue for Christians is not whether they should be involved in politics or contend for laws that affect moral behavior. The question is how."[79]

However, that battle has been waged by so few for too long. In the current compass bearings of the United States, the Church has been largely acting as if she doesn't know how to use a compass and thereby is marginally effective, if at all, for the map of the United States. A more aggressive form of political action is now unquestionably necessary.

This aggressive action can have a very positive mode to it. Ed Silvoso is a man trained in both business and theology with substantial experience in both. Although from a "Charismatic" bent, he has developed a strategy outlined in several books but finds its culmination in the book Ekklesia. *This book both outlines a strategy of aggressive action to help governmental entities to become more effective in what they do, reduce crime, and economically prosper. He documents its effectiveness over time by video documentaries, and has caught the attention of National Geographic and the New York Times, just to name a few. The transformational strategy is global in its vision and has seen results of cultural and governmental transformation in many different countries. His work of applying the Temporal Mandate in a positive mode has proven effective. But make no mistake, this movement is comprised of bold, risk-taking Christians who have defied the status quo and passionately follow their King.* [80]

Francis Schaeffer, in his book *A Christian Manifesto*, has a chapter entitled "The Use of Force." He outlines political action to be that force to be contended with which cannot be ignored nor brushed aside: "Our representatives must be confronted with political force," and "The State must be made to feel the presence of the Christian community" are the level of aggressive political action that is necessary for the Church to be responsible to their King [81] Charles Colson, a formidable warrior in politics as a Christian citizen, sees the political arena in which the Christian community has no option but to win, stating,

> Christians have an obligation to bring transcendent moral values into the public debate. All Law implicitly involves morality; the popular idea that "you can't legislate morality" is a myth. Morality is legislated every day from the vantage point of one value system or another. The question is not whether we will legislate morality, but whose morality will we legislate.[82]

Please hear this! These profound Christian thinkers who make such assertive statements and sound the alarm for the Body of Christ are notable and well-respected men and women both by the Church and in the secular world. If we are armed with the rational, Biblical passion of aggressive political action, it is inevitable that civil disobedience will and must follow.

Fighting-Stage 2: Civil Disobedience

Civil disobedience is ever present within the Scriptures. Biblical examples have been spiritualized and reduced to past relics within the "Sunday school"-ish comforts of the Church. A small sampling of three examples follow: The Hebrew midwives refusing Pharaoh's command to kill innocent children (Ex.1:16f); the three Hebrew young men refusing to worship an idol and Daniel's refusal to obey the king's order not to pray to YHWH (Dan. 3 and 6, respectively); and the Apostles' refusal to obey the governmental order to quit preaching the resurrected Christ (Acts 4:18, 5:29).

In an ethical analysis of civil disobedience within the Scriptures by God's people, Norman Geisler gives a conclusive and useful rule of thumb from the Scriptures: "No Christian has a *social* obligation to obey a government which assumes the place of God. On the contrary, the Christian has a *spiritual* obligation to disobey such a government." [83] This same passion should be visible in how we relate to our culture which is in revolt against the King. You see, sometimes the most Godly action you can take in your walk with Jesus Christ, your King, may land you in jail! That's food for thought in your Sunday morning worship.

Throughout Church history, our spiritual ancestors repeatedly wrestled with Scripture and found a bottom line in which they believed they had no choice but to actively disobey government or run counter to many in their culture. Starting with the example of Christ, whose crime from Rome's point of view was that of civil insurrection ("King of the Jews" was nailed to His cross, naming the crime of capital punishment), Schaeffer releases a panorama of heroes of the faith who were guilty of civil disobedience: Christians being thrown to the lions, people like Martin Luther, William Tyndale, John Knox, Samuel Rutherford, and hundreds of others are but droplets in the ocean of the tens of thousands of Christians who suffered for their obedience to Christ the King by disobedience to civil authorities.[84] Volumes have been and much more could be written of such examples of loyalty to Christ over earthly kings.

Schaeffer then concludes with fiery zeal, "But when *any office* commands that which is contrary to the Word of God, those who hold that office abrogate their authority and they are not to be obeyed. And that includes the state. The *bottom line* is that at a certain point there is not only the right, but the duty, to disobey the state." [85] Civil disobedience is not about mere political viewpoints. It is a calling out of authority and an aggressive means of being "salt and light" to the state on behalf of God's Word. Ever the diplomat, Colson gives a clear disposition to this force: "Rightly exercised, civil disobedience is divine obedience. But when Christians engage in such activities, it must be to demonstrate their submissiveness to God, not their defiance of government."[86]

Sometimes, civil disobedience may not actually be civil disobedience. The disposition of this written call to action is that of informing the Christian citizen first so that, second, they are in a place of instructing government about God's will for the Church-state relationship. However, in many cases, government officials—including police officers, school officials, mayors, etc.—may be ignorant of the Law and seek to deny or prosecute Christians who are acting in a manner well within the law. Nonetheless, these misinformed officials will perceive those actions to be "civil disobedience," when, in fact, they are not. Such can be the case when Christians may picket, demonstrate, display signs or Nativity scenes, or any open display and action of Christian conscience. Such ignorance gave birth to the "American Center for Law and Justice," of which Jay Allen Sekulow is chief counsel. In a handbook entitled *The Christian, the Court, and the Constitution*, he lights the fires of aggressive political actions and public demonstrations by Christians, actions that may be perceived as civil disobedience, by admonishing, "It is time for Christians to go on the offensive and have our voices heard." [87] The entire handbook, however, is an informational legal guide about laws that do allow such aggressive actions in the public (and sometimes private) square but for which Christians, in particular, are being prohibited, abused, sued, and even jailed for.

What must be stated here very clearly is that the Church indeed must "go on the offensive and have our voices heard" and to challenge the *status quo* of our culture, whether it is ignorantly legal (Jay Sekulow's disposition) or unjustly illegal (the Biblical examples' depiction). Dr. Richard Land was a professor of mine who used to state an axiom, "We fight for what is right, not because we will win but because it is right!" I would humbly modify Dr. Land's dictum for our Biblical context by stating, "We fight for what is right, not because it is legal, but because it is right!" In doing so, there will be punitive consequences which we must be willing to pay. "We must practice the truth even when it is costly."[88]

Isaac Backus was a Baptist clergyman, Church historian, and descendant of the *Mayflower*. Because of his adamant stand for Christian liberty, along with his fellow Baptists, they "were repeatedly fined, whipped and incarcerated for faith-related offenses."[89] Their sacrifices due to civil disobedience won the day to bring about the First Amendment to the Constitution of the United States. Their actions and consequent sacrifices joined the pages of historical heroes of the Christian faith, and also paved the way for the greatest and longest lasting statement of religious liberty in history. Did you hear that? There would be no First Amendment were it not for their sacrifice!

The line has been drawn in the sand since the beginning of time. From a Biblical point of view, for the Christian citizen the question can never be, "Should we ever practice civil disobedience?"

> If there is no final place for civil disobedience, then the government has been put in the place of the Living God, because then you are to obey it even when it tells you in its own way at the time to worship Caesar. And that point is exactly where the early Christians performed their acts of civil disobedience even when it cost them their lives. [90]

The questions may be "How?," or "When?" perhaps, but never "If."

Fighting Stage 3: The Defensive Use of Force

Hold on to your guns now, literally! We return to the Biblical doctrine of the use of deadly force by the people of God to the application of revolution against a government who has "crossed the line" against God. Francis Schaeffer, in many ways, was a revolutionist. A Christian pastor, theologian, philosopher, and prolific writer, yes, but he was a revolutionist throughout.

He envisioned a time in which the people of God would need to draw a bottom line and, ranging from aggressive political action to civil disobedience, would need to act, sometimes with armed force. "When discussing force it is important to keep an axiom in mind; always before protest or force is used, we must work for reconstruction." [91]

However, his impatience with our Christian pacifism and "wimpiness" of Christianity in our Country this last century brought him to frustration to say,

"The whole structure of our society is being attacked and destroyed. It is being given an entirely opposite base which gives exactly opposite results. The reversal is much more total and destructive than that which Rutherford or any of the Reformers faced in their day." [92] "What then is the Christian response? The Christian, it is assumed is to choose reconciliation. But we cannot have reconciliation in a world like ours unless something happens first…no nice soft talk of reconciliation and the content less word *love* is going to have any meaning in such a setting. We must have something stronger. We must have a Christian revolution." [93]

Many could not imagine that Schaeffer, the famous philosopher and theologian, could mean "revolution" literally. However, the examples he uses in his texts cite actual, armed revolution such as when he discussed Rutherford's *Lex Rex*, John Knox and other Reformers, and even the historical context of the United States Revolutionary War. Schaeffer undoubtedly had armed conflict as a possible necessity in mind.

Schaeffer is far from being alone in his Biblical conclusions on this subject. Charles Hodge is but another example of many who would use the word *resistance* and *revolution* in the context of when the people of God must draw the proverbial line in the sand with government, or with society:

"This is obviously right. The right of resistance is in the community. It is the right of revolution, which God sanctions, and which good men in ages past have exercised to the salvation of civil and religious liberty. When a government fails to answer to the purpose for which God ordained it, the people have a right to change it." [94]

Even the ever-cautious statesman Charles Colson admits, "So, for the Christian, revolution is never to be lightly regarded. It is the most extreme form of disobedience. It could only be contemplated on the same justification as a just war; that is, there must be a better alternative as a result of a revolution." [95]

There are many theologians, Biblical exegetes, Christian philosophers, and statesmen who assent to revolution with force, either explicitly or implicitly by the use of arms. Somehow, in my education, we used these same textbooks, but conveniently passed over chapters or words such as these in order to get to what was seen as priority 1: spiritual evangelism. The spiritual mandate was heralded in our classrooms, and thus in our pulpits, at the cost of the cultural mandate, which was on the very same pages equally espoused by these spiritual mentors in our required reading list.

Historically, these two mandates are not in opposition to one another, even as admitted by Jonathan Kaufmann in the *Wall Street Journal*, "It was the Great Religious Awakening two and one half centuries ago that helped sow the seeds of the American Revolution." [96] We have already noted the historical documentation that these two mandates, the eternal and the temporal-cultural, work hand-in-hand with each other, just as God has designed it. This is true, even if force is used, because we have established that God is not against His people's use of force, as long as it is righteous in His eyes.

Samuel Rutherford, in his book *Lex Rex*, answers this question of "*WHETHER OR NOT THE LAWFULNESS OF DEFENSIVE WARS HATH ITS WARRANT IN GOD'S WORD*," by giving a Biblical argument for force against government. Based upon the examples of David, Elisha, and the eighty priests who resisted King Uzziah, etc., he argues the uses of force was a posture against an offensive act or acts of evil and is warranted, and even the obligation of His people to take up arms, if necessary, against the "king." [97]

The purpose of this book is not to answer all the fine nuances of precisely when and under which specific circumstances God's people are to take up arms. My only goal is to establish that there is a Biblical precedent for the use of lethal force, if necessary, to defend one's life, one's family, and one's neighbor. There is a Biblical and Church historical precedent for God's people to take up arms in defense against a government or culture that has revolted against God, if not in their covenantal, constitutional, or moral obligations.

Again it must be absolutely clear that the Christian ethic and worldview is not to be against government, as it is an established institution by God Himself. Anarchy is an abomination to God. Rather, the Church collectively and the Christian citizen individually, seek not to overthrow government in a revolution but to replace those governmental leaders who have abrogated their authority by such aggrievances against God and man. Even Dietrich Bonhoeffer, who in his younger years wrote, "According to Holy Scripture, there is no right to revolution,"[98] would later revisit his erroneous ivory-tower statement during the reality of Hitler's terrorism and instead, become a revolutionary spy to personally attempt to assassinate Hitler. Under Biblical conviction he did join a counterrevolution, and under Biblical conviction, he would hang for his assassination plans and attempts against the tyrannical Third Reich governmental leader, Adolf Hitler.[99] When you hear the often quoted phrase "Cheap grace," it was Bonhoeffer who coined the term in referring to Christianity apart from sacrifice.

Samuel Adams, one of the Founding Fathers, in a treatise entitled "The Rights of the Colonists as Christians," intended to defend the religious liberty that King George was stripping away from the Colonies before the Revolution. He ominously warned,

> These (religious rights) may best be understood by reading and carefully studying the institutes of the great Lawgiver and Head of the Christian Church, which are to be found clearly and promulgated in the New Testament. That great author, that great jurist, and even that court writer Mr. Justice Blackstone, holds that this recognition (of religious liberty) was justly obtained of King John, sword in hand. And peradventure it must be one day, sword in hand, again rescued

and preserved from total destruction and obliv-
ion." [100]

Are we in that state as a country right now? At the time of
this writing, I think not, only because we currently have a president, Donald Trump, who, however imperfect he might be, at least
"tips his hat" toward godly values in government affairs. However,
we must be prepared for the worst, and pray it never happens, but
prepared we must be.

Throughout Scripture and Church history, men and women
of God have struggled with a Biblical view and consequent action of
integrity under God so as to honor Him with the use of force, in differing measures, against government or anarchist-type mobs. Many,
like Bonhoeffer, turned from pacifist to aggressive revolutionist to
use deadly force offensively against an evil government. Others have
used the lesser force of forceful civil disobedience against government
and resorted to arms, only to defend their lives and property against
government when threatened. Generally, the latter was the premise
of the American Revolution.

In truth, the British began the revolution against the Colonies.
The Colonies responded with a counterrevolution of defense: the
American Counterrevolution. However, make no mistake, the impe-
tus of Scripture and of Church history is that God has called His
people to be a counterrevolution against society's revolt against Him
by being His "salt and light" agents. It is His desire to see cultures
transformed, yes, with the Gospel of eternal transformation, but
equally so by His Kingship over all men, in the here and now.

"Make disciples" goes hand in hand with "You are salt and
light." "You must be born again" embraces Peter's civil disobedient
declaration; "Whether it is right in the sight of God to give heed
to you rather than to God, you be the judge." It is the Christian's
responsibility as ambassadors of the King to instruct government
on their mutual responsibility to put God, the King, first. It is the
Church's duty to demonstrate the ultimate King's authority by the
use of aggressive political action and civil disobedience, and even the
use of armed force, if necessary, to defend life, and to suppress evil,

even if it must be against government or mobs bent on harming you, your family, or your neighbor.

> Why are the nations in an uproar,
> And the peoples devising a vain thing?
> The kings of the earth take their stand
> And the rulers take counsel
> Against YHWH and His Messiah:
> 'Let's get free of God!
> Cast loose from Messiah!'
> The One enthroned in the heavens laughs,
> The Lord scoffs at them.
> Then He gets good and angry.
> Furiously, He shuts them up:
> 'Don't you know there's a King in Zion?
> A coronation banquet is spread for Him on the holy summit.'
> Now therefore, O kings, show discernment;
> Take warning O judges of the earth.
> Do homage to the Son,
> Lest He become angry, and you perish in the way.
> (Psalm 2:1–6, 10, 12)

CHAPTER 5

Citizens' Line in the Sand
Your Surprising Boundaries
toward Government

Sacred Boundaries: Submission To God-Given Authority

N ow how in the world can a boundary of submission to government be surprising? Read ahead and get your heart pills ready. As we investigate the Biblical teaching of a citizen's boundaries toward their government, we will find the boundary of submission to authority is a sacred one. What is surprising is the prioritization and order of submission is God, home, Church body, and, lastly, to civic government.

This simple Biblical imperative is an argument from the greater to the lesser. One is to be in submission to God and His Word. Within that submission, one will find their proper role of submission within the home, the Church and toward government, in that order.

To keep this simple, we will only address the relationship of the citizen to the government. Therefore, the relationship of authority within the home and within the Church will be discussed only in how it relates to the secular government boundaries, and not deal with a Biblical teaching on home and Church per se.

The Home Authority

"No institution on earth is more sacred than that of the family. None is more basic. As is the moral and religious atmosphere in the family, so will it be in the Church, the nation, and society in general."[1] This was written by William Hendriksen in his commentary on Ephesians. God's Word sees governmental authority beginning in the first created institution, the home. The order of society and government begins with the home and is the womb of understanding authority under God. To use a sports illustration, submission to God's authority is "home base." Submission to authority in the home is "first base." Following is submission to authority in the Church as "second base," and "third base" is its application to secular government.

If we take the passages in Ephesians 5:22–6:4, we will see that the argument of authority and obedience is based upon the nature of the Godhead and replete with wholesome, compassionate, and loving order, but order and government it is. The participle from 5:21, "Be submitting to one another—"υποτασσομενοι" within the Body of Christ is borrowed over into the command to wives in 5:22, "wives, be submitting (υποτασσομενοι) to your own husbands as to the Lord." That's a participle along with the verb, "υποτασσεται" in 5:24 and with the imperative, "υπακουετε" in 6:1, all address order, or governmental roles within the family. Each of these words begin with the preposition, ῦπο, signifying, "under power, rule, sovereignty, command" when used in this manner.[2] This is precisely true of the injunctions used by Peter (1 Pet. 3:7) and elsewhere by Paul (Col. 3:18 ff.).

It is important to note that within this warm cocoon of nurturing proper order within the home, that authority is not a cold, harsh dictatorship. Paul will balance the clear authority of the husband with the imperative "Love your wife" and in relation to the children, "Do not provoke your children to anger." All this is within the larger context of Christ's authority over us, along with His self-sacrificial love and His giving of Himself to us.

Peter, likewise, contextualizes Godly authority within home by ordering, "You husbands likewise live with your wives in intimate understanding, show her honor as a fellow heir of the grace of life" (1 Pet. 3:7). "Subject in all things does not mean, however, that she is in the hands of one who has authority to command what he pleases. Her subjection…is such that she can never find grievous or humiliating."[3] Since the home is the world's "first base" of practicing godly authority, it can be extrapolated that God's attitude of proper authority in the home, Church, and even government is not to be a cold, harsh, and inhumane bludgeon by a ruthless dictator. Rather, it is order and submission within the atmosphere of compassion, love, and understanding and seeking the best for those under one's authority. Therefore, our first boundary line with government is to practice authority and submission within the home, so that society learns godly and proper submission to the State's authority. If a home, however imperfectly, practices loving authority, so will those members properly understand and submit to what should be government's humane and selfless authority.

It is in the government's best interest then, that the citizen nurtures a home of respectful, caring submission to authority within the home. Such is the stabilizing foundation for any society and nation. It may perhaps sound altruistic, but governmental leaders should be seeking God's will for the design of a family, and not some socially engineered paradigm doomed for failure. Church and State should be working hand-in-hand to encourage a father-and-mother home, and to discourage the breakdown of God's pattern for a home; to assist the family with its proper boundary of loving authority within the home. This is God's will for the family, and the government should duly encourage it for its own sake. Hear this clearly! To the degree that family is operating in a healthy manner is the degree to which the health will be government and society.

The current smoke screen of attempting to redesign sexual identities is well within this same discussion of what the government should protect the family from. If the government wishes to preserve itself, it should advance the clear creation design of the sexes and of the definition of family. This is your challenge: you should demand no less from your government.

Accordingly, God's people should once again revisit and encourage this godliness in the home. Dr. Curtis Vaughn, a man I remember to be of great tenderness yet also of very high ideals in this area, quoted Elton Trueblood's clarion call for the home to rise up agai:, "Of all the disintegrating factors the chief is the loss of the sense of meaning of what a family ought to be. Our basic failure is not the failure to live up to the standard that is accepted, but rather the failure to keep the standard clear." [4] This "standard" is the boundary of loving authority within the home.

These are "fighting words": whenever an arbitrary, abusive authority steps out of line with God's will in the home that authority is to be disobeyed. The same is true of the citizen toward governmental abuse of power. However, that scenario has already been addressed in chapters 1 and 2.

The Body of Christ Authority

You will find this perhaps disturbing or interesting. When we venture into the arena of submission to Church authority, the Biblical data is not as clearly defined as are the other two authorities of home and state. One passage only appears to be clear when it commands, "Obey your leaders, and submit to them" (Hebrews 13:17). However, the exegesis of this verse is more telling than is commonly understood and has been greatly misunderstood and abused.

First of all, this passage is clearly within the context of the author addressing a Christ-believing community. However, the *sitz em leben*, or "situation at hand," is critical to understanding this call to submission to Church leadership authority. The writer to the Hebrews is addressing a particular situation at a particular time:

> "*Having exhorted the Hebrews to keep in mind their former rulers and adhere to their teaching, the writer now admonishes them, probably in view of a certain mutinous and separatist spirit encouraged by their reception of strange doctrines, to obey*

their present leaders, and yield themselves trust-
fully (υπεικετε) to their teaching—an admonition
which, as Weiss remarks, shows that these teachers
held the same views as the writer." [5]

Dods simply points out that this "Obey and submit" to Church
leadership in this case has to do with the call to the Body members to
place themselves under doctrinally pure teaching from the Word, and
away from factitious heresy and practice. These leaders, whose teaching
was known to the writer of Hebrews, were approved by and apparently
met true Biblical teaching standards with the Hebrew writer. This pas-
sage is within a historically contextual focus. In an attempt to make these
verses comprehensible to laity, Foy Valentine argues that this was "advice
providing unqualified endorsement of the leaders in a particular fellow-
ship of Christians to whom the letter was originally sent... They rightly
divide the word of truth... They are "apt to teach" (2 Tim. 2:24, KJV)[6]

This verse is written to Hebrew-Christians who were in danger
of reverting to a heresy of syncretism or returning to their Jewish
background entirely. This analysis of the Hebrews passage is not to
entirely deny authority by godly leaders, but only to point out that,
in context to this passage, the obedience and submission seems to
be limited to the leadership's instruction and guidance in matters of
doctrine from the Word. This is the shocker: Church leaders who
are not doctrinally sound and masters of the Word, or "apt to teach,"
have no authority in the Body of Christ in God's eyes!

Another passage from Ephesians alluded to earlier in discussion
of family government is Ephesians 5:22, in which the Apostle Paul
is giving pastoral guidance to the Church for harmony and order,
"and be subject to one another in the fear of Christ." *The locative*
of sphere, "in the fear" (εν φοβω), combined with the subjective gen-
itive "of Christ" (Χριστου), is critical to understanding this passage.
The mutual submission of the members of the Church toward one
another (which includes the pastoral leaders) stems from a proper
understanding and healthy respect, (or "fear") before the Head of
the Church. Within the proper order and exercise of spiritual gifting
toward one another for mutual benefit (vv. 18–20), there is a rec-

ognition of Christ's authority and rule that should result in mutual submission. Orderliness, mutual respect, and self-government are the order of the day within the Body of Christ.

What can be concluded is that there is a "government" that operates within the Church. Some of the spiritually gifted members have an authority that comes from their Biblical ability and skill to instruct and teach under Christ, which their titles signify ("overseer," "pastor," "elder"). There is also a self-governing that is to take place within the body of Christ as well. Overall, the "government" scope within the Church appears to be much narrower than that which is to be in place in the home. Nonetheless, it does exist, and the boundary of proper submission to that Church body government is to operate under the submission to Christ's lordship. Again, what cannot be lost is that the authority which is delegated to the Church body leadership is an authority which is (1) based on their skilled use and application of the Word for the body, and (2) set in the context of loving "watch care" over the body. Their authority has the boundaries and limitation to able instruction in the Word, and that, with unlimited expression of love.

In summary, the citizen's dutiful boundary to government is to be under submission to Christ, in proper submission within the home, and in obedience to God's Word in the Church. All this governance within the God-given institutions is the foundation to a proper perspective of what it means to be in submission to secular government, the last of God's institutions. Each governmental institution created by God (family, Church, and secular government) has the boundary of using their authority to seek the best interest of those under them.

The Secular Government Authority

Finally, we come to "third base" in our baseball analogy. We have explored the priority levels of governmental roles in order of Biblical importance: first, under the government of the Christ, the King (or simply "God"), which is "home base"; secondly, under the government of the home, which is "first base"; and thirdly, under the government of the Church, which is "second base," and now finally, under the government of the State which is "third base." Obviously, to a nonbeliever, the second base of Church authority does not exist. The duty to submission to the State presupposes proper submission to previous priorities, and in that paradigmatic order. The citizen's duty to secular government must begin by its duty to the others first, and in proper prioritization, at least from a Biblical point of view.

It is unnecessary to elaborate about the Biblical role of the Christian citizen's obligation to secular authorities at this point since that has already been discussed in chapters 1 and 2. The Biblical commands to "be in subjection to governing authorities" (Romans 13:1) and "Submit yourselves for the Lord's sake to every human institution" (1 Peter 2:13) have been already explored. However, it does bear repeating that, from the Christian citizen–secular government point of view, this is a clear and positive boundary the citizen has with the secular government. *"The claim of government, which is based on its power and mission, is the claim of God and is binding on conscience. Government demands obedience 'for conscience sake' (Rom. 13:5), which may also be interpreted as 'for the Lord's sake' (1 Pet. 2:13)."* Subjection/submission to the State is the presupposing attitude and positive boundary ordered by God, unless it is in a violation of God's order, as determined earlier.

The Authority of Constitutional Contract

I will bet you didn't see this one coming. This order of Biblical boundaries is equally true of the social contract between the citizenry (that's you and I) and the state. Explored in earlier chapters, God expects both the State and her citizens to submit to the terms of that social contract, as He takes contracts very seriously. In other words, as it pertains to the United States, both government officials and the citizens of the United States have an obligation before God to be in submission to the Constitution of the United States of America. It is a standing covenant you chose to swear to or were born under. The citizen, Christian or not, has a God-given boundary to not encroach upon the government further than agreed upon in the US Constitution. A citizen, or a coalition of citizens, cannot expect nor demand its government to act unconstitutionally in the same way that government is expected to not act unconstitutionally either. This has already been ascertained from a Biblical point of view in previously in this book.

The Dangerous Work of Drawing These Boundaries Carefully

Since you are reading this book, you have endeavored to dig deep into God's Word into understanding His heart and mind on profound matters. Armed with this knowledge, you must be careful about using this powerful knowledge with skill. There are important distinctive truths you must use with your growing knowledge.

The Biblical Map of Our Country Is a Map, but Not a Theocracy

You, the Christian citizens, are placed in what appears to be a conflicting dilemma of respecting proper boundaries between its obligations to God and the State's authority under God. On the one hand, the citizen is obligated to be responsible to the King of kings who expects His Kingdom citizens to further His Kingdom in this world: the "Temporal Mandate." This we explored in chapter 1. Then, on the other hand, the Christian citizen's King at the same time expects of His servants to maintain the proper and separate institutional boundary of the State. The Kingdom citizenry are delegated to be "salt and light" invading the world, including the State. This was explored in chapters 2 and 4.

Yet at the very same time, God has created the separate distinct institution of the State, with its set boundaries around it. This apparent clash of these two spheres is the stuff of which Christendom has struggled for centuries. It was also the debate fodder of the American Founding Fathers' struggle to create the American Experiment. Since the scope of this chapter is the Christian citizen's boundary from the government (that is, the Church's proper boundary it has with the State), we will focus solely on what the Church is not supposed to inject into the State. The question really is, how far does God expect our being "salt and light" into government need to go? How does God expect us, as best as can be derived from Biblical data, to maintain the distinction of the State yet work to keep it account-able before God? While holding the State accountable, what is our God-given boundary toward secular government? I believe a proper Biblical understanding of the Christ-given Temporal and Eternal Mandates are unquestionably imperative to keep a balanced admin-istration of the two. Too many Christians have faulted in being igno-rant of God's balance with these commands to us. Now, what follows are some more "fighting words."

The Church Is Responsible to Build God's Temporal Map into Government

The "Temporal Mandate" to God's people, being the "salt and light" to the world, has already been explored and elucidated at length in chapter 4 and in the introduction of chapter 1. That Temporal Mandate is the historical "map" of our Country that we are to responsibly build into our governments.

Indeed, you cannot forget that Christ, the King, expects His Kingdom citizens to have an impact upon society and government. He is given "all authority in both heavens and earth" (Matt. 28:18). As that King of kings, He properly defines the source and definition of "Law," which is transcendent above man in authority. His citizens are expected to keep government in line with that understanding of Law, *or to put it as John Calvin did, "Yet this distinction (between Church and Government) does not lead us to consider the whole nature of government a thing polluted, which has nothing to do with Christian men."[8] As it pertains to the United States of America, in Biblical revela-*

tion, the American Founders discovered that a "system of absolutes exists upon which government and Law can be founded."[9] The foundational base from which to derive and define laws of men was "God's written Law, back through the New Testament to Moses' written Law; and the content and authority of that written Law is rooted back to Him who is the final reality."[10]

When government is told by God's Kingdom citizens who it is that defines Law, conflict can very well arise. With the early formation of the Church, we see the tension fomenting. "Herod feared Christ because He represented a Kingdom greater than his own. Christians were martyred not for religious reasons but because they would not say, 'We have no king but Caesar', the Roman government saw them as political subversives." [11] Who it is that defines Law is critical to the results within society and the world. A passing example is when the Supreme Court of the United States made an absurd and evil decision to declare slaves "chattel" in the 1859 Dred-Scott case, thus defining certain human beings as mere property. Within our own Country, those who wish to change the Constitutional nature of our government and moral base have neither rights nor legitimate powers to do so, no matter their political title or power as senator or congressman or Supreme Court Justice.

If we are to understand what the Church, as part of God's Kingdom, is to be responsible for, it is to be proactive agents of defining Justice and Law to our governments and to hold that ground in our society. It is to expect and demand from government and neighbor what God expects from them. Being "salt and light" as it pertains to our governmental relationship is to be unapologetically transformational in these areas. The "Temporal Mandate" or "Cultural Mandate" means we are ambassadors of a God over the universe that is both its Creator and Supreme Law Giver, and Who it is that gives order to society and government. This is a critical distinction from the "Eternal Mandate" of God's people in which we bring people to know Christ through the Gospel.

These two mandates must not be confused; these two agendas must not be mixed, lest we dishonor God's boundaries between the two. While the citizens of God's Kingdom are to impose the

Temporal, Cultural Mandate on government, we cannot expect to impose the Eternal Mandate on a temporal, cultural order, such as government, even if it is a created institution of God. In simpler terms, we are to legislate God's morality; however, we cannot legislate God's eternal salvation onto government or ask government to do so.

The Church Is Not to Impose of the Eternal Mandate onto Government

Since God's Word has revealed to us that government was "established by God" (Rom. 13:1), we find that this institution is God's intention to establish order in society within this temporal realm. The role He gave the Church to spread the good news and to make disciples for eternity's sake is not meant to be imposed upon government. Even while Francis Schaeffer defends the Christian's use of force against government within the United States when it violates God's will for it, he then makes clear,

"First, we must make definite that we are in no way talking about any kind of theocracy…the American Founders had no idea of a theocracy. This is made plain by the First Amendment…We must not confuse the Kingdom of God with our country. To say it another way, 'we should not wrap Christianity in our national flag.'" [12]

In short, the Christian citizen is not called to make the government like the Church, nor should she even hope to do so. French theologian Jacques Ellul eloquently spoke to this careful distinction:

> Thus he (the Christian) must plunge into social and political problems in order to have an influence on the world, not in hope of making it a paradise, but simply in order to make it tolerable-not in order to diminish the opposition between this world and the Kingdom of God, but simply in order to modify the opposition between the disorder of this world and the order of preservation

that God wills for it-not in order to "bring in" the Kingdom of God, but in order that the Gospel may be proclaimed, that all men may really hear the good news of salvation through the death and resurrection of Christ. [13]

The Body of Christ, created for eternity and for serving God's Kingdom on earth, has the God-given boundary to not impose the Eternal Mandate upon the temporal institution of government. The Temporal Mandate of bringing truth and Justice and Righteousness to government, yes, but the Eternal Mandate, no! Should these lines become confused, dire consequences occur. *For instance, Colson documents the history of the Constantine Empire in which these distinctions became entirely blurred. He depicts how even Augustine was seduced into the Church/State union so that he endorsed state suppression of Christian heretics (thereby defying his own "City of God"/ "City of man" roles). While Constantine's legalization of Christianity in AD 313 helped to end Christian persecution, the tables were turned, and the Church/State became the torturer and persecutor of non-Christians equally evil and grotesque as their persecutors had been.[14] This is a mark of shame in the Church's history and is the result of the Church not honoring her God-given boundaries with government.*

This Church/State confusion was a large part of why the American Founders envisioned and produced the First Amendment. From the history of Constantine to their recent Church of England experience, among others, they sought not a restriction of Godly influence upon the United States Government but any "establishment of religion" by our Government. *The following excerpts by some of our Biblically influenced Founding Fathers show that this idea of wanting a nation of Biblical consensus would also mean restricting the Church from certain "boundary breakers" before God. James Madison, hailed as the "Father of the Constitution," was educated at Princeton under the tutelage of the Presbyterian theologian John Witherspoon and a fellow signer to the Constitution. He became fluent in Biblical Hebrew, which would have given him the world view of Biblical Law.*

Despite the debates over James Madison's personal religious convictions, he displayed the conviction of a Biblical paradigm for Law and saw a Biblical consensus in his political views and influences. In his "Memorial and Remonstrance against Religious Assessments," he argued against Christian compulsion enforced by the state. This resolution appealed to Christian citizens that Christianity's own teachings precluded politically coerced support:

> *"We hold it for a fundamental and undeniable truth, 'that religion or the duty which we owe to our Creator and the manner of discharging it can be directed only by reason and conviction, not by force or violence.' Whilst we assert for ourselves a freedom to embrace, to profess and observe the Religion which we believe to be of divine origin, we cannot deny an equal freedom to those whose minds have not yet yielded to the evidence which has convinced us. If this freedom be abused, it is an offence against God, and not against man: To God, therefore, not to man, must an account be rendered." [15]*

To paraphrase Madison in a succinct manner, he believes God will judge the Church for unBiblical imposition (of the Eternal Mandate) upon the State, a violation of a boundary between the Church and the State. In a similar vein, Isaac Backus, the Baptist minister and Founding Father, argued against any kind of religious test for public office: "Nothing is more evident, both in reason and the Holy Scriptures, than that religion is ever a matter between God and individuals, and, therefore, no man or men can impose any religious test without invading the essential prerogatives of our Lord Jesus Christ."

During the course of this debate (over Biblical Church and State separation), religious liberty becomes the cornerstone of *e pluribus unum*—"out of many, one."[16] The Westminster Confession of 1646, predating the American colonies by a hundred years, nailed the issue of proper coercion of faith in God's hands alone by stating, "God alone is Lord of conscience."[17] In these sample excerpts out of so many others, we see a judicious view by the Founding Fathers of maintaining a delicate balance between a Biblical consensus of the people's government and a boundary for the Church to not trespass, namely that of state-sponsored religion (Madison) and a religious test for public office (Backus). We must note very carefully, however, that this struggle for a Church-State balance reveals the very genius of our Founders and the resulting Documents of our nation. Within the American Experiment, we have as healthy a respect for both institutions as any government in world history. This is one of the reasons that our Constitution is the longest lasting in world history.

It is out of this Biblical history of our nation, the Judeo-Christian consensus, that runs through the very ink of her founding documents and into the very soul of this nation, that the God-given "awkward dance" takes place. Like my independent wife and I who wrestled through ballroom dancing, each struggling to take the lead in the dance which portrayed an unsure awkward dance, so God has chosen the two dancing partners of Church and State to step on each other's toes in their dance. Sometimes, it can look like a beautiful dance of love, but much of the time, it appears more like a grueling wrestling match. Nevertheless, as my wife and I dance, we did because we are in a covenantal relationship. Apparently, while the dance floor of this temporary world exists, God has matched these two unlikely partners to dance with each other, and dance we will, until He stops the music of time, or whenever the Church abandons her mission and walks away from the dance floor. Already, we seem to have been heading this shameful way. But I, and hopefully you, still believe in the Church's resurrection.

The question really lies in the Church's understanding of her responsibility and obligation to dance, no matter how uncooperative, stubborn, or forceful the other partner gets. Through our King's Temporal Mandate, we are under orders to dance. Time and eternity are in the balance of our obedience. Will you, your Christian friends and family walk away from the dance floor in defiance to your King? I think not!

The Balance Keeper: Mutually Raised Swords

The Sword of the Government

Although I have used the humorous word picture of the "awkward dance" between my wife and me to depict the struggle between two God-given institutions, it is obvious that the reality of that power struggle is much more serious. We have previously concluded that the State only has a derived authority from God or, quite literally, "under God." *After Romans 13:1 commands our subordination to governing authorities (υποτασσεσθω), the rationale is then given, "for there is not an authority if not under God (ει μη υπο θεου). The Christian citizens place themselves "under" ("υπο") civil authority because civil authority is "under" ("υπο") God.* The power and use of force by the government is derived from, and under, God. It is a derived authority with Biblical responsibilities and boundaries.

The Sword of the Church

At the same time, we have also clearly concluded that the Church, acting as an agent for Christ's Kingdom, has a derived authority from God. We have asserted that from Christ's authority ("given to Me all authority in heaven and upon the earth," Εδοθη μοι πασα εξουσια εν ουρανω και επι της γης; Matt. 28:18), He has delegated to the Church the authority to "make disciples" and to be "salt and light" to the world, which includes governmental systems. The power and use of force by the Church is derived from, and operates under, God. It is a derived authority with Biblical responsibilities and boundaries.

Therefore, both the State and the Church have delegated authority from God that have designs and limitations from God. Furthermore, the proper use of force by each is also derived from God's authority. Although there are some Christians who believe the Church does not have the authority to use "force," I have thoroughly investigated the systematic Biblical theology and have concluded otherwise (c.f. the introduction in chapter 1). Herein is "the rub"; two institutions from God, both delegated with authority, both permitted to use "force" under God to perform their duties under God. Both will inevitably be at odds with each other: the State must punish evil, but the Church upholds God's definition of evil; the State is to bring Justice for its citizenry, but the Church imposes into government God's paradigm of Justice; the State is to bring order to society, but the Church mandates the equal value and dignity of all human beings no matter their station in life.

The bottom line from a theological point of view is that mutual force between the two becomes the balance keeper in society. Both are to keep the other accountable before God: the State in her civil authority, the Church in her Kingdom authority.

This relationship of the Church and State does not have to be solely antagonistic, however. Although Bonhoeffer writes from his context of European Germany in the 1940s, he promotes congeniality between government and the Church. While reminding us that government does not possess the office of confessing and preaching faith in Jesus Christ, government should not pursue a Christian policy, enact Christian laws, etc. For the sake of their common Master, the Church claims to be listened to by government; she claims protection for the public Christian proclamation against violence and blasphemy; she claims protection for the institution of the Church against arbitrary interference; and she claims protection for the Christian life in obedience to Jesus Christ. [18]

The government should be a friendly protector of the Church, while not being a promoter of the Church. The Apostle Peter commands, "Honor the King" (1 Pet. 2:17), in the context of the promotion of a healthy society. It is not outside the imagination of a godly citizen to be a cheerleader to the government when it promotes Justice, Righteousness, and good as God defines them (c.f. also Rom. 13:1–10). The dance may indeed be awkward; however, it does not mean the dance cannot also be congenial and civil, and perhaps even amiable at times.

The sovereignty of God has ordered this awkward dance within a fallen world. He apparently sees the necessity of both in a world made up of societies of both fallen, sinful humanity and His called-out people from among them while they struggle and fight for God's good for society. It is a de facto reality that government as the State will wield its authority upon her citizens. The critical and seminal issue at hand is, does, and will the Church wield its God-given authority within society and upon government? More to the point, as His ambassador, will you? Are the people of God, His Church, acting in loving obedience to their King by enforcing their right upon the State? Will the Bride of Christ be as righteously angry and act in force as their Groom did when He saw gross inJustice permeating into His society?

The King has given us a Mandate to be a formidable force in society under His authority. He has called His people to action to transform society and to fight for His Kingdom, "on earth, as it is in heaven." Will the Church abandon her mission from God or be His faithful ambassadors? It is time for us, particularly in this time within the United States, to pick up our sword and to act fearlessly.

Right now, I ask you to acknowledge your King and ask yourself, "Will I?" Only if your answer is a "Yes!" to your King, then turn to this last chapter. If your answer was "No!" to your King, then I ask you to put this book down and walk away, just like Peter did initially in his denial of Christ. He wants only men and women who can pledge allegiance to the King of kings with their lives to take the next step.

CHAPTER 6

A Godly Call to Arms
(Do NOT read this chapter if
you are not prepared to fight!)

Introduction

At the onset of this work, I had stated that that I have hopes to ignite a revolution among God's people to become the transforming army of God for His sake, and for posterity's sake. I know from Church history that the Body of Christ can be re-awakened—set on fire, if you will—to become the formidable Kingdom ambassadors that are respected and feared because of the King they represent and follow at any cost. I can see signs of an awakening already.

However, we are now in that pivotal moment in our American history. The side of evil and hatred for the God of the Scriptures is very much showing its face in our Country, even as I write this final chapter. The bullies who hate our Biblical map and compass for our Country are acting out with no fear of God or His people. They have no idea of the slumbering giant they are stirring up. They believe you, the Church, and all with a moral compass are but a fairy tale for silly people. God has birthed His people during this generation, "for such a time as this," to borrow from the Book of Esther. It is time for God's giant to arise with a roar and flex its muscles. You wonder why

God has you in this Country, where you live and why He has blessed you so? To make His history happen now!

This is no idle talk. The exegesis and teaching of Scripture can become intellectual idolatry if it does not lead to God's Spirit convicting, transforming work that leads us into repentance and action. The "call to arms" of this section is directing the reader to be prepared to hear their King's heartbeat and heed His call to "take up your cross and follow Me" (Matt. 16:24, NIV).

A Godly Call and Declaration of War

When we speak of being an "offensive force," we are not talking about being rude, crude, or not showering. We are cleaning up our identity of who we are, really are, before our God and Savior. What must be quickly repeated before we proceed is that the Scriptures—that is, our King—fully supports a proactive, protective disposition against evil in our culture. This was investigated in chapters 1 and 4 but is stressed here pointedly.

The best way to put it is how Russell Moore, president of the Ethics and Religious Liberty Commission of the Southern Baptist Convention stated it: "The Kingdom of God is a declaration of war." [1] Did he mean by this statement that we are to take up assault weapons against culture and government? Not primarily, although that is a legitimate last resort for us. More to the point, Dr. Moore cries out to the Church to be the undefeatable, transforming, and optimistic force in culture: "The Kingdom's advance is set in motion by the Galilean march out of the graveyard. We should then be the last people to skulk back in fear or apathy…we do not despair as those who are the losers in history might. We are the future kings and queens of the universe." [2]

Today, the Western Church has fallen victim to the "Taming of the Shrew" mentality in Shakespeare's play. Where once pastors were the military leaders of their congregations in our Country's beginnings, so many are but paid hirelings hoping not to offend the tithers until retirement age. The American Church has largely bought into the lies of the enemy through our culture that Christianity is to be passive, inoffensive, seeking not to "rock the boat." We are expected to be the compliant wife of our environment and government. We are commanded to be submissive to "Lord Culture," lest it beat us back in our "place" at its feet. At worst, we are tolerated be a snarling nuisance, a toothless, barking dog on the porches of our Churches better laughed at, then engaged.

The Biblical position, the disposition to our culture (including government) that our King has called us to is quite contrary. The Bible does not assume a pacifist disposition of Christ's followers. Within chapter 1, this writer has sought to exegete Christ's command in Luke 22:36 to "buy a deadly weapon for defense." The graphic imagery of Jesus's cleansing of the Temple and using a "whip," a weapon of force that may well have drawn blood, to strike out at beast and man was created by the same Lord who could say, "Blessed are the peacemakers." To view our God, our Lord, our King and Savior as a pacifist is contrary to His revealed Word. "To impose a nonviolent or pacifist grid on the words and actions of God/Jesus requires significant hermeneutical gymnastics—an approach that creates an interpretive straitjacket."[3] To quote Dr. John Jefferson Davis, "The pacifist tradition is based largely on a literal interpretation of the sayings of Jesus. Such a hermeneutical approach is difficult to maintain consistently."[4] Although these passages are about self and civil defense, the point is that God and His people are not pacifists in any sense of the word.

This declaration of God's desire for His Church to be a force on the offense in this world does not negate the virtues of grace, forgiveness, love and gentleness and the Fruit of the Spirit that is to be evident within the Body of Christ. These Godly virtues, however, are not in contrast but in harmony with He Who said, "I will build My Church, and the gates of Hades will not overpower it" (Matt. 16:18). These words are in the context of a battlefield. Jesus expects His Bride to be a force that the enemy must engage. Being "salt" is a preservation catalyst, but it is also a stinging salve to a putrefying wound. Being "light" can mean hope and joy in darkness. On the other hand, it can be painfully blinding, like a tactical flashlight blazing to the eyes of culture and government in the darkness. Forcefully engaging our culture and our government with the King's Rule of Law is the most loving act of love to our culture.

The point of this section is not to exhaust what has already been stated in earlier chapters. It is simply to remind ourselves that the Church, the Body and Bride of Christ, is meant to be a formidable force within our environment. The better picture of the Church is that of a preacher who causes riots (Paul) or Apostles who defiantly oppose wrongful government mandates (Peter and his cohorts). This is because of their Leader who preached messages that can get one killed and Who with force acted out righteously on "Church" property (Jesus). The Biblical imagery time and again, not just in the Old Testament but pervasive throughout the New Covenant, is that of a battlefield, of soldiers, of a winning team that can never truly die or lose in its struggle against evil in every level of culture.

The Church in God's Kingdom has a, "blessed hope" worth sharing to the world, and worth dying for in the process. We are a battleship engaging the enemy and caring for the wounded while setting sail for our eternal inheritance. We are not a cruise ship oblivious to the islands of decimation all around us. God has called us to be a force on the offense for His "already, but not yet" Kingdom.

A Godly Call to Being a Force Within Our Culture

Where then is this battle to take place? Is this battle a cutesy picture on a Sunday school flannel board of an iconic soldier fighting some snarling, pitchfork-carrying, red-suited character? It is easier, frankly, for the Church to spiritualize the Christian life into an adult version of the flannel-board mentality. It is less troublesome to go to a Bible study on spiritual warfare and limit the battle to our own persons. This is a very good start, but only a start. It is safer to sit within Sunday school walls and memorize the weapons of warfare than to actualize them at the voting booth, in a Starbucks conversation, or a public show of force at City Hall or the State Capitol building.

Although this writer certainly believes in, and has worked with, the demonic realm individually and corporately, it is easier to limit the battle to one's self and to deny the call to engage those same forces working within our culture. In an interesting note to this point, the author watched a newscast interviewing a witch who had declared war against President Donald Trump by calling all witches to cast spells upon him. Amanda Garcia, the head witch and "Oracle" of a large coven in Los Angeles, stated that President Trump's "mean actions were intended to hurt her and those she cares about." She stated she was seeking to unite all witches against him to "galvanize people to resist him for the greater good of society so that we can have a whole, healthy world."[5]

One can see the "angel of light" (2 Cor. 11:14) mirroring, for evil purposes, the precise call of our King to be a united force for the good and health of society as He, not the enemy, defines it. Indeed, we are called to spiritual warfare as a Body of Christ, but it is applicable not only to one's self but also to the armies of Satan mounting themselves against our culture and government. This battle is not "either/or," it is "both/and."

Chapter 4 delineates exegetically from Scripture our King's call to be "salt and light" to our culture and to government. This work has illustrated through Church history and the American experiment's pathology how the obedience to engage the world as salt and light has transformed peoples, nations, and governments. Presently, our Western Church and American history shows a nation crumbling from within because of the missing, united force of the Church. Dr. Larry F. Johnston stated this grievous omission pointedly:

> "While the corrosive forces of postmodernism, relativism, consumerism, hedonism, materialism and scientism are more than adequate to explain the progressive spiritual and moral deterioration of any nation not illumined by a Christian worldview and "salt-ified" by at least a righteous remnant living among its citizens, I'm mystified; where are the opposing forces? I hear the bleating of sheep. But where is the roar of our lions?"[6]

A quick glimpse over our shoulders into recent Church chronicles will hear the history-changing John Wesley warn, "There is no holiness but social holiness" and to make it "into a solitary religion is to destroy it." [7] Individually and collectively, we are called to be transformers of culture around us and government above us. *When in Matthew 5:13 and 14 Jesus addressed the nascent Church, He addressed them in the plural, "Υμεισ εστε το αλασ τησ γησ...υμεισ εστε το φοσ του κοσμου...";* "You all are the salt of the earth... You all are the light for the world." The Church is to be a united army, a collective force to make the real difference. Too long and too selfishly we have made too much of doctrinal distinctions at the price of cultural death cries of agony, the equivalent of "polishing brass on a sinking ship." "Are we so obsessed with defending the theological distinctive dear to our individual doctrinal tribes that, with eyes fully riveted on our navels, we fail to see the growing armies of belligerent secularists firmly intent on silencing our witness once and for all?"[8]

Our King's Inescapable Call to Be the Church Militant

The "call to arms" of this chapter is directing the reader to be prepared to be within the hearing distance of their Savior's calling to "take up your cross and follow Me" (Matt. 16:24, NIV). Although this call by Jesus is set in the historical setting of a Judaic world that meant ostracization from family and society if one were to follow Jesus, the application to our present cultural atmosphere may well call for a high price in following His Temporal Mandate. It may mean giving our heart, time, and financial resources to positively change our culture and her institutions, including government. It may mean the adventure of being a heavenly ambassador could cost us physical or financial pain as we confront the forces of evil and draw a line in the sand with hate-groups intent on representing their king, Satan. It may mean we must be willing to go to jail for obeying our King in defiance to governmental kings. That would be civil disobedience, just like the Apostle Peter, the other Apostles, and the heroes of our faith did.

However, the fulfillment and the joy in this world and beyond of being such an agent for Christ and His authority, we are promised, are well worth it. The shining testimonies from the persecuted Church herald this reality. Of course, Paul would anticipate with us the future blessings, "For I consider that the sufferings of this present time are not worthy to be compared with the glory that is to be revealed to us" (Rom. 8:18). Which of us do not covet to hear the words "Well done, good and faithful servant..." (Matt. 25:23, NIV), when we see Him face-to-face? Truly, this is a goal worth living, working and dying for.

There are, however, rewards that are tangible now. There are the rewards of seeing our streets safer for our children, our grandchildren, and us. There is the joy of being part of government transformation, not only in history but also in our present day, as will later be documented. There is deep satisfaction in being a part of the creation of a society in which open dialogue of Christianity's values flourish in a culture of truth, liberty, and Justice. There are the many multifaceted joys of living in a Country where God is at least honored by the president and, more importantly, where the citizens propagate the King's values, whether they recognize them as His or not.

We reap such blessings for now and eternity when God's people are living with their ear on their King's heart and their feet in the footprints of Him surrounded by His "cloud of witnesses" (Heb. 12:1). This book distilled from the Scriptures and particularly this chapter is a call to arms to do so. The "arms" we employ may be a positive, transformational work in our institutions; it may be massive, organized civil disobedience; and yes, it may even be literal weapons as a last resort to protect ourselves, our families, and our property, all of which I have endeavored to Biblically argue for in this work. It all begins with a heart of repentance, a mind changed to hear the Master's voice.

Repentance from "Churchianity"

The above words should be alarming to most. I would submit that those words are shocking because we, especially in the Western Church, are guilty of "Churchianity":

- We can read the Hallmark of Fame of those who suffered and died for their faith in God in Hebrews 11 and teach them in the comfort of a Church wall.
- We can listen to stories from our home DVD player (and, case in point, no longer available in our public school rooms) of the American Fathers who pledged their lives and fortune to give birth to a godly nation.
- We can subscribe to magazines like "The Voice of the Martyrs" that document our brothers and sisters in the modern-day lion's den all over this world, even to this very moment.

Still, we can be alarmed and offended at a "call to arms" from the Scriptures, from our living King. To the Church's very beginnings, and yesterday and today in much of the world, such words are not shocking. The King's call to arms were and are the considerations of their daily life. To us in the Western Church, we may be alarmed because we have baptized ourselves into a culture of "Churchianity."

Christianity has been falsely portrayed to be comfortable, good sermons and warm feelings, entertaining worship with songs we prefer, and, above all, hell-fire insurance. We have believed the deception that the Church is a cruise ship in which we engorge fine foods, instead of Jesus's design of a battleship engaging the gates of hell.

Paul's Point of View on "Churchianity," from Romans 12:1–3

There is some insight the Apostle Paul shares with us about how the Church needs to break loose of "Churchianity." When he addressed the Roman Church about the non-conformation of spiritual worship, in verse 2, Paul implores us to "not be conformed to this world." The word world is the Greek word αιώνι, or "age." Paul uses the other Greek word κοσμοσ (cosmos) elsewhere when he wants to depict an inherently evil world system. Here, he does not use that word denoting an evil system per se, but a less morally incriminating word.[9] We are not to be "pressed in the mold," συσχηματιζεσθε, or "be schematized along this 'age'" literally.

So coming back to Paul's use of the word age *in v. 2, and in the context of chapter 12, particularly in verses 3–8, he is not imploring us to not be conformed to an "evil system," the "world," but rather to not be pressed into a mold of the status quo, of a geographical "Bible Belt" or any other culture; this "age."* Eugene Peterson, in his Message translation brilliantly illuminated the Apostles Paul's verbiage and thought:

> Don't become so well-adjusted to your culture that you fit into it without ever thinking. Instead, fix your attention on God. You'll be changed from the inside out. Unlike the culture around you, always dragging you down to its level of immaturity, God brings out the best in you, develops well-formed maturity in you." (Rom. 12:1–2, The Message).

Having been a pastor, I recognize another tradition of this "age," a "sacred cow" among Christians that can be conscience inoculation against being "salt and light" to our culture around us; "Churchianity" prayer. A Biblical view of prayer by nature is to include action as well as prayer.

I appreciate the power of prayer; I have seen its effectiveness in my own life. However, such a mentality can be a cop-out. It is easy to say, "I'll pray for you," then go home and sink into an easy chair and watch television. The Church is holding "the truth in unRighteousness" when the Church remains silent on the issues and fails to act as the Bible requires.[10]

Again, I would be very careful to point out that Biblical prayer is the breath of the Church's life. However, I have seen too often God's people use prayer as an inoculation of their conscience from action. James put it wryly, "'Go in peace, be warmed and filled,' and yet you do not give…what use is that? Even so, faith, if it has no works, is dead" (James 2:15–16, NASB). Prayer, without works to back it up, is a corpse. Prayer, with hard work and a warrior's disposition, is the breath of life into a valley of dry bones.

In colloquial terms, Paul, under the inspiration of the Holy Spirit, is commanding us to not be a flock of "sheeple" created by those around us, whether it is our surrounding secular culture or within the inbred Church cultural habits that may defy His marching orders. It is upon us now. We are now at the crossroads of becoming an impotent instrument in the hands of God if we continue our traditional pathways of Churchianity. You perhaps know who George Barna is. Read his frightening words:

> America's emerging culture, driven by its politically correct attitudes and a passion for silencing Christianity displayed by numerous liberal power brokers, has sucked the spiritual oxygen out of our society. Are Christians willing to do what it takes to reverse this trend? The smart money says the answer is "no" for the foreseeable future. It is more likely that growing numbers of believers will acquiesce to pressure to keep their beliefs private.[11]

The phrase "Keep their beliefs private" is Barna's statistician statement of Christianity's refusal to obey the Temporal Mandate. The lies of the past that "religion and politics" are not discussed in polite circles and are private matters has had its full fruition in a society that cannot recrucify Christ, but can certainly muzzle and beat down His followers. However, I do not share in Barna's seeming pessimism. The sleeping giant may still be sleeping but if awoken can flex his muscles triumphantly throughout culture, for we, the giant, serve a Giant King.

Conclusion

There is one clear, pertinent application of this passage to the modern Church. In Church history (for that matter, even in the Old Testament), the people of God repeatedly become stagnant. Because of an ingrown tendency to become their own subculture within their culture, they end up adopting their cultural compass around them either in part or in whole "baptizing" those adaptations as if they were the "Biblical standard" and solely God's will for the Church.

Dietrich Bonhoeffer is an example of one who chose not to be conformed to the "age" of thinking that swept the European Churches, who almost unwittingly fell into Hitler's fascism. What would a Church congregation say today about their pastor's execution for attempting to assassinate their national leader? No doubt the majority of the modern Church today would write Bonhoeffer off as a madman who couldn't possibly have been a Christian. Now, our history honors him as a hero and martyr of the Christian faith.

As one who has been in and around evangelical Christianity almost his entire life, I argue that this is the case today for the Western Church we live among. Surely you cannot help but to see the parallel between the "Churchianity" of Nazi Germany's Churches and the "Churchianity" infecting the modern Western Church.

A short story told to Penny Lea by a German Christian during the Nazi Regime helps to document what was happening to the Churches in Germany, and how it might shed light on our own "age" today.

"Sing a Little Louder"

I lived in Germany during the Nazi holocaust. I considered myself a Christian. I attended Church since I was a small boy. We had heard the stories of what was happening to the Jews, but like most people today in this country, we tried to distance ourselves from the reality of what was really taking place. What could anyone do to stop it?

A railroad track ran behind our small Church, and each Sunday morning we would hear the whistle from the distance and then the clacking of the wheels moving over the track. We became disturbed when one Sunday we noticed cries coming from the train as it passed by. We grimly realized that the train was carrying Jews. They were like cattle in those cars!

Week after week that train whistle would blow. We would dread to hear the sound of those old wheels because we knew that the Jews would begin to cry to us as they passed our Church. It was so terribly disturbing! We could do nothing to help these poor miserable people, yet their screams tormented us. We knew exactly at what time that whistle would blow, and we decided the only way to keep from being so disturbed by the cries was to start singing our hymns. By the time the train came rumbling past the Church yard, we were singing at the top of our voices. If some of the screams reached our ears, we'd just sing a little louder until we could hear them no more. Years passed and no one talks about it much anymore, but I still hear that train whistle in my sleep. I can still hear them crying out for help. God forgive all of us who called ourselves Christians, yet did nothing to intervene.[12]

We can sit around comfortably within the confines of four walls on Sunday morning or stand on our spiritual laurels, singing louder or using microphones to preach loud enough to drown out the screams of our American culture around us. The "Holocausts" of rampant abortion, same-sex marriages, transgenderism, sexual-identity "crises," gangs proud to be anarchist wreaking havoc on lives and property while police officers stand by are just a few examples. These symptoms can be laid at the feet of a Church that has chosen to be "nice and kind and spiritual," and not truly Christ-following and confrontational with God's Justice. We have bowed to a false view of God by writing off His Justice and, therefore, His love for the world's good. We have sold an emasculated Christianity.

What then is the Christian's response? Some Christians have supposed that the choice is between a revolutionary stance and some kind of reconciliation. But we cannot have reconciliation in a world like ours unless something happens first. We are headed for the disaster I have described above, and no nice, soft talk of reconciliation and the contentless word *love* are going to have any meaning in such a setting. We must have something stronger. We must have a Christian revolution. God is not only a God of love but also a God of holiness. He is a God of character.[13]

As to these tendencies of God's people to "conform to this age" or what I would call "Churchianity" in this context, our God has always been faithful to break up this pattern by sending persecution and then revival and reformation to His people. A glimpse of God's hand into the early Church was in Acts 11:19, and then in Acts 18:1, when He sent a persecution from Rome to get the Church's stagnation out of Jerusalem. Throughout our Church history, God has used leaders who "think outside the box" (not "conformed to this age") to chart a different course for His people. This is His "gift of grace to some" as displayed in the overriding theme to the Book of Romans.

We can see small brave pockets of renewal and reformation beginning to happen today, but it is needed badly on a wider scale. Those lonely soldiers don't need just reinforcements, they're needing the entire army to show up! We are being called to the battle! We can see the evil counterrevolution against many actions of godliness in the news every day. We must pray and must act so that it will not require the persecution that is seen in Church history and presently around the globe. We must become as respectfully bold and defiant to government and culture as our heroes of our faith were.

The Church must remember that she is not the child of the world around her but princes and princesses called to represent the King of the universe. The people of God must quit acting like slaves of government, content to live quietly on their Master's plantation and instead remind their government they are freedmen who are here to subpoena them to the King's Court. Remember who you are. God's Bride will someday sit with their Groom to judge angels.

> "It's our turn to march into the future. The pursuit of Righteousness and Justice is of no purpose if it doesn't flow from seeking the Kingdom first.

Beside us, there are many flags, and we'll pledge allegiance where we ought and where we can. But over, always over us, there's a cross. We may not always see where we are going, but we know the Way. Onward." [14]

A Godly Call to Action

This concluding "Godly Call to Arms" is meant to be succinct, pointed, and an alarm to the people of God to fulfill their destiny by the Hand of God upon them, or to simply "fade to black" in relative insignificance.

Dare not to be a "sheeple." An unknown source has stated, "The greatest illusion the Church can be under is that they are thinking they are 'doing something' when they are actually doing nothing." What defines our calling and legacy as God's Hand in this world is not what our families, Churches, and cultures says it is or what it ought to be, but what the King's marching orders are.

Remember that Our God is a very great God doing very great things around us and throughout the world to fulfill His plan. Jesus said, "My Father is working right up to this very moment, even so I am working" (John 5:17, my translation). His words are the paradigm of our cooperative work with God. Our King is in the business of calling out His people for eternity, and in the business of making His "Kingdom come, His will be done" in society and government. We but have to open our eyes to see His Ruling Hand working miraculous feats through His people both here and globally. Ask God to open your eyes to how greatly He is at work already, and be encouraged by that to jump in with both feet! Will you join the triumphant march of His victorious army or go AWOL from your King and His battle?

Join in on the legacy of God's people who are listening to their King's marching orders, rolling up their sleeves, and being part of miraculous transformation in the world. Dr. Cliff Daugherty, an educator who is turning public school systems on their heads in

California by implementing Kingdom principles, said, "We are God's army who specialize in the "Repo Market"; we are taking back possession what the world has stolen!"[15] The "Transform our World" movement is largely composed of the Charismatic Church. Still, this movement of brave, fighting soldiers consists of modern-day heroes.

A source documenting this transforming force of God's people globally is Ed Silvoso's book *Ekklesia*. In it he states, "It may surprise you to hear what God loves the most is not only the Ekklesia. And when we embrace everything that He loves, it radically changes for the better the way we see and do ministry as His Ekklesia. "'Outreach ministries" become "in-reach ministries" because the "congregation" just became citywide."[16]

It may appear that there are two competing Biblical models of fulfilling our role as the Church in seeking both the Eternal Mandate and Temporal Mandate from our King. On the one hand, there is what has been elucidated from Scripture throughout this dissertation as what I would call, "Confrontational Model," in which God's people takes their delegated authority from Christ the King in drawing a "line in the sand" between God's Law and our culture's and government's morphing of "law." On the other hand, we can see a growing movement among God's people to obey the Temporal Mandate by choosing to befriend and invade government[262] and culture by transforming it through Kingdom principles of business, education, and the marketplace.

I believe that these are not competing Biblical models but complementary ones. We begin with the "Transformational Model" in hopes of making a radical difference in the atmosphere of government and society. However, if the Transformational Model is rejected or suppressed, the Confrontational Model becomes the modus operandi of the Church.

In either case, the call to arms from our Savior and King is clear: whether by loving transformation or loving confrontation, the people of God must rise up and act on their faith lest it be a "dead faith." God has created a people, and has recreated His people for "such a time as this." We are in the crosshairs of history. God has placed His people here. God has placed you here. He is on the move. He calls you out to be the heroes of the King.

Will you shrink back in cowardice? We both know the answer to that question for you, don't we? You, the history maker; you, the royalty of the King; you, the warrior and hero of your Hero...

MARCH FORTH!

BIBLIOGRAPHY

Alexander Balmain Bruce. The Expositor's Greek New Testament, Vol. 1, the Synoptic Gospels: Matthew. Edited by W Robertson Nicoll, Grand Rapids, Michigan: Eerdmanns, 1983.

Alexander, Ralph H. The Expositor's Bible Commentary, "Isaiah, Jeremiah, Lamentations, Ezekiel." Edited by Frank E. Gabelein. Grand Rapids, Michigan: Zondervan, 1986.

Arnn, Larry P. The Founders' Key. Nashville: Thomas Nelson, 2012.

Barclay, William. The Daily Bible Study Series, "The Gospel of Matthew." Philadelphia: Westminster Press, 1975.

Barna, George. America at the Crossroads: Explosive Trends Shaping America's Future. Grand Rapids, Michigan: Baker Books, 2016.

Bauer, Walter. A Greek-English Lexicon of the New Testament and Other Early Christian Literature. Edited by Revised and Augmented by F. Wilbur Gingrich and Frederick W. Danker. Second ed. Chicago and London: University of Chicago Press, 1957.

Blaiklock, E.M. Tyndale New Testament Commentaries: The Acts of the Apostles, R.V.G. Tasker, Gen Editor. Grand Rapids, Michigan: Wm. B. Eerdmanns Publishing Company, 1974.

Blair, Edward P. The Layman's Bible Commentary. 25. Richmond, Virginia: John Knox Press, 1964.

Bonhoeffer, Dietrich. Ethics. S. C. M. Press, Ltd. translation ed. New York: MacMillan Company, 1955.

Brown, H. Tertullian's apology; Or Defence of the Christians, against the Accusations of the Gentiles. London: Tho. Harper, 1655.

Bruce, Alexander, W. Robertson Nicoll, General Editor, The Expositor's Greek New Testament, Vol. 1. Grand Rapids, Michigan: Eerdmanns, 1983.

Bruce, F.F. The New International Commentary on the New Testament: The Book of Acts. Grand Rapids, Michigan: Wm. B. Eerdmans Publishing Company, 1979.

Calvin, John. Institutes of the Christian Religion. Vol. 2, 3. Philadelphia: Westminster Press, MCMLX.

Church, Forrest. The Separation of Church and State. Boston: Beacon Press, 2004.

Cole, Neil. Organic Church: Growing Faith Where Life Happens. San Francisco: Leadership Network, 2006.

Colson, Charles W. Kingdoms in Conflict. Grand Rapids, Michigan: Zondervan Publishing House, 1987.

_____. Loving God. Grand Rapids, Michigan: Zondervan, 1983. Congress, 106th and 2d Session. "What Is the Purpose of the U.S. Government?" Our American Government (2000, Washington).

Congressional Research Service. Respectfully Quoted. Washington, D.C: United States Government Printing Office, 1989.

Copan, Paul, and Matthew Flannagan. Did God Really Command Genocide? Grand Rapids, Michigan: Baker Books, 2014.

Cornell University Law School. "Oath of Office", 5 U.S. Code 3331. Legal Information Institute.

Dana, H.E., and Julius R. Mantey. "Comparative Clauses." In A Manual Grammar for the Greek New Testament. 1955. Reprint, Toronto, Ontario: MacMillan Company, 1927.

Daugherty, Cliff. "Quest Institute Quality Education Center," 27th Annual Transform our World Global Conference. October 12, 2017.

Davis, John Jefferson. Evangelical Ethics: Issues Facing the Church Today. Phillipsburg: P&R Publishing, 2015.

Dods, Marcus. The Expositor's Greek Testament: The Epistle to the Hebrews. Edited by W. Robertson Nicoll. Grand Rapids, Michigan: Wm. B. Eerdmanns Publishing Company, 1983.

Editors of Encyclopedia Britannica. "Authoritarianism, Politics." Encyclopedia Britannica Inc., online edition.

Eichrodt, Walther. Theology of the Old Testament, Vol 1. Philadelphia: Westminster, 1959.

Ellul, Jacques. The Presence of the Kingdom. New York: Seabury Press, 1967.

Erickson, Millard J. Christian Theology. Grand Rapids, Michigan: Baker Book House, 1988.

Foulkes, Francis. Tyndale New Testament Commentaries. Edited by R.V.G. Tasker. Grand Rapids, Michigan: Eerdmanns Publishing Company, 1963.

Geisler, Norman L. Ethics: Alternatives and Issues. Grand Rapids, Michigan: Zondervan Publishing House, 1971.

George, Robert. Why We're Losing Liberty. Princeton: Princeton University, 2016.

Grudem, Wayne. Systematic Theology. Grand Rapids, Michigan: Zondervan, 1994.

Hendriksen, William. New Testament Commentary: Exposition of Ephesians. Grand Rapids, Michigan: Baker Book House, 1979.

_____. New Testament Commentary: Exposition of the Gospel According to Mark. Grand Rapids, Michigan: Baker Book House, 1975.

Henry, Carl F. H. Christian Personal Ethics. Grand Rapids, Michigan: Baker Book house, 1979.

Hillsdale College Politics Faculty. Constitution 101: The Meaning and History of the Constitution. 2015. Accessed July 4, 2017. http://online.hillsdale.edu/course/con-101.

_____. The U.S. Constitution: A Reader. Hillsdale, Michigan: Hillsdale College Press, 2015.

Hodge, Charles. Systematic Theology. 3 vols. Grand Rapids, Michigan: Wm. B. Eerdmanns Publishing Company, 1981.

Hogue, James, and Ebbie C. Smith. Christianity Faces a Pluralistic World. Fort Worth, Texas: Christian Literary Publications, 1989.

Johnston, Larry F. "At the Crossroads." Christian Research Institute: Life and Truth Matter (August 2017). http://www.equip.org.

Katheryn Pfisterer Darr. The New Interpreter's Bible, "Ezekiel",. Nashville: Abington Press, 2001.

Keil, C.F., and F. Delitzsch. Commentary on the Old Testament. Peabody, Massachusetts: Hendrikson Publishers, 1989.

Kleck, Gary. Targeting Guns: Firearms and Their Control. New Jersey: Rutgers University: Transaction Publishers, 1997.

Knowling, R.J. The Expositor's Greek New Testament, Vol. 2: The Acts of the Apostles. Grand Rapids, Michigan: Eerdmanns Publishing Company, 1983.

Koyzis, David. "Is It Time for American Citizens to Disobey Government?" Christianity Today, March 8, 2016. http://www.christianitytoday.com.

Lane, William L. The New International Commentary of the New Testament. Edited by F. F. Bruce. Grand Rapids, Michigan: Eerdmanns, 1974.

Lea, Penny. Sing a Little Louder. Accessed August 27, 2017. Abstract retrieved from http://www.internationalwallofprayer.org/A-010-Holocaust-Memorial-Day-Stover.html.

Lean, Garth. Strangely Warmed. Wheaton, Illinois: Tyndale Publishers, 1979.

Lewis Sperry Chafer. Systematic Theology, Vol.7. Dallas, Texas: Dallas Seminary Press, 1940.

Lomasky, Loren. "Contract, Covenant, Constitution." George Mason University, Online Edition.

Mary Frances Owens. The Layman's Bible Book Commentary. Nashville: Broadman Press, 1983.

Metaxis, Eric. Bonhoeffer: Pastor, Martyr, Prophet, Spy. Nashville: Thomas Nelson, 2010.

Moore, Russell. Onward: Engaging the Culture without Losing the Gospel. Nashville, Tennessee: B & H Books, 2015.

Newman, Barclay M. Jr. A Concise Greek-English Dictionary of the New Testament. Stuttgart, West Germany: Wurttemberg Bible Society, 1971.

Rutherford, Samuel. Lex Rex: Or, the Law and the Prince. Glasgow: Edinburg: M. Ogle & Son and William Collins, 1644, Reprinted 1843.

Schaeffer, Francis A. A Christian View of the Church. Westchester, Illinois: Crossway, 1982.

_____. A Christian Manifesto. Westchester, Illinois: Crossway Books, 1981.

_____. The Church at the End of the Twentieth Century. Westchester, Illinois: Crossway Books, 1982.

Schaeffer, Franky. A Time for Anger. Wheaton, Illinois: Crossway Books, 1982.

Sekulow, Jay Allen. The Christian, the Court, the Constitution. Virginia Beach, Virginia: American Center for Law and Justice, 2000.

Silvoso, Ed. Ekklesia. Minneapolis, Minnesota: Chosen-Baker Publishing Group, 2017.

Spence, H.D.M. The Pulpit Commentary: 2 Chronicles. Edited by Joseph Excell and H.D.M. Spence. Electronic Database: Hendrikson, 1990.

Strassel, Kimberly. The Dark Art of Political Intimidation. n.p.: Wall Street Journal, 2016.

Summers, Ray. Essentials of New Testament Greek. Nashville: Broadman Press, 1950.

Tackett, Dale. "The Truth Project: Vol. 1, What Is Truth? DVD-ROM. Focus on the Family. Colorado Springs, Colorado: Focus on the Family, 2006.

The National Association of Chiefs of Police. "17th Annual Survey of Police Chiefs and Sheriffs." The Police Times, 2005.

The Pulpit Commentary: 2 Chronicles. Edited by Joseph Excell and H.D.M. Spence. Electronic Database: Hendrikson, 1990.

The U.S. Congress, U.S., 106th, and 2d Session. "What Is the Constitution?" Our American Government (2000, Washington).

The U. S. Constitution. Edited by Hillsdale College Politics Faculty. Hillsdale, Michigan: Hillsdale College Press, 2015.

The United States Supreme Court. Bowers v. Devito, 686 F. 2d, 616, 7th Cir. Accessed 1982. http://casetext.com.

The Westminster Assembly. The Westminster Confession of Faith. Carlisle, Pennsylvania: Banner of Truth Press, Broadcast in 1647.

Tucker Carlson Tonight, "Witches Cast Spells on "Wicked" Trump," Fox News, September 19, 2017, 5:01 PM.

Valentine, Foy. The Layman's Bible Book Commentary: Hebrews, James, 1 & 2 Peter. Nashville: Broadman Press, 1981.

Vaughn, W. Curtis. The Letter to the Ephesians. Nashville: Convention Press, 1963.

Von Rad, Gerhard. Old Testament Theology, Vol 1. New York and Evanston: Harper Row, 1965.

Whitehead, John W. The Second American Revolution. Westchester, Illinois: Crossway Books, 1982.

Wright, James D. "Armed Criminals in America: A Survey of Incarcerated Felons." U. S. Bureau of Justice Statistics: A Federal Firearms Study (July 1985).

Wright, James, and Peter Rossi. Armed and Dangerous: A Study of Felons and Their Firearms. Harry Ransom Humanities Research Center; The University of Texas at Austin: Aldine, 1984

ENDNOTES

Introduction

1. "Blame Trump's Victory on College Educated Whites", The New Republic, Nov. 15, 2016. "Behind Trump's Victory: Division by Race, Gender and Education", Pew Research Center, Nov. 29, 2016. "7 Charts Show Who Propelled Trump to Victory", Business Insider, Nov. 10, 2016.
2. Russell Moore, *Onward* (Nashville, Tennessee: B & H Books, 2015), p.49

Chapter 1

1. Russell Moore, Onward (Nashville, Tennessee: B & H Books, 2015), pp 66,.67
2. Charles Colson, *Kingdoms in Conflict* (Grand Rapids, Michigan: Zondervan Publishing House, 1987), 530.
3. Dale Tackett, "*The Truth Project: Vol. 1, What is Truth?*" Focus on the Family.
4. John Whitehead, *The Second American Revolution* (Wheaton, Illinois: Crossway Books, 1982), 20.
5. Whitehead, *American Revolution*, 20.
6. Whitehead, *American Revolution*, 120.
7. Whitehead, *American Revolution*, 112.
8. Ibid., 31.
9. Whitehead, *American Revolution*, 21.
10. Schaeffer, *Manifesto*, 430.
11. Whitehead, *American Revolution*, 77.
12. Colson, *Kingdoms*, 368.
13. Franky Schaeffer, *A Time for Anger* (Wheaton, Illinois: Crossway Books, 1982) 62.
14. John Calvin, *Institutes of the Christian Religion*, vol. 2, 3 (Philadelphia: Westminster Press, MCMLX), 848.
15. Schaeffer, *Manifesto*, 430.
16. Dietrich Bonhoeffer, *Ethics*, trans. S.C.M. Press, fifth ed. (New York: Macmillan Company, 1955), 339.
17. Ibid., 336.

18. Calvin, *Institutes*, 1493.

19. Colson, *Kingdoms*, 532.

20. Whitehead, *American Revolution*, 76.

21. Whitehead, *American Revolution*, 48.

22. Schaeffer, *Manifesto*, 468

23. Larry P. Arnn, *The Founders' Key* (Nashville: Thomas Nelson, 2012), 3.

24. Congressional Research Service, Respectfully Quoted (Washington, D.C: United States Government Printing Office, 1989), 343.

25. Whitehead, *American Revolution*, 33–34.

26. Whitehead, *American Revolution*, 28-32.

27. Schaeffer, *Manifesto*, 28-32.

28. Ibid. 432.

29. Arnn, *Founders' Key*, 8.

30. Whitehead, *American Revolution*, 432.

31. Ibid., 74.

32. Schaeffer, *Manifesto*, 435.

33. Forrest Church, *The Separation of Church and State*, (Boston: Beacon Press, 2004), 14.

34. Norman L. Geisler, *Ethics: Alternatives and Issues* (Dallas: Zondervan Publishing House, 1971), 158–   177.

35. Geisler, *Ethics*, 171

36. Paul Copan and Matthew Flannagan, *Did God Really Command Genocide?* (Grand Rapids, Michigan: Baker Books, 2014), 302.

37. Copan and Flannagan, *Genocide?*, 44.

38. William Barclay, *The Gospel of Matthew: Volume 1* (Philadelphia: Westminster Press, 1975), 166.

39. Alexander Balmain Bruce, *The Expositor's Greek Testament: Volume 1* (Grand Rapids, Michigan: Eerdmanns Printing Company, 1983), 112.

40. Copan and Flannagan, 47.

41. Colson, *Kingdoms*, 346.

42. Copan and Flannagan, *Genocide?*, 306.

43. Copan and Flannagan, *Genocide?*, 300.

44. Ibid., 42.

45. John Calvin, *Institutes, Vol. 2*, 1,499.

46. Colson, *Kingdoms*, 584.

47. Eric Metaxas, *Bonhoeffer: Pastor, Martyr, Prophet, Spy* (Nashville, Tennessee: Thomas Nelson, 1987), 358–404.

48. Copan and Flannagan, *Genocide?*, 310.

Chapter 2

1. Erickson, *Christian Theology* (Grand Rapids, Michigan: Baker Book House, 1988), 641, 642.

2. Alexander Bruce and W., *The Expositor's Greek New Testament, Vol. 1* (Grand Rapids, Michigan: Eerdmanns, 1983), 79.

3. Wayne Grudem, *Systematic Theology* (Grand Rapids, Michigan: Zondervan, 1994), 863, 864.

4. Charles Colson, *Kingdoms in Conflict* (Grand Rapids, Michigan: Inspirational Press, Zondervan Book House, 1987), 340.

5. Lewis Sperry Chafer, *Systematic Theology, Vol.7* (Dallas, Texas: Dallas Seminary Press, 1940), 177, 178.

6. Colson, *Kingdoms*, 347.

7. Dietrich Bonhoeffer, *Ethics* (New York: Macmillan Company, 1955), 332.

8. Charles Colson, *Loving God* (Grand Rapids, Michigan: Zondervan, 1983), 167.

9. Francis Schaeffer, *A Christian Manifesto* (Westchester, Illinois: Crossway Books, 1981), 468.

10. Hillsdale College Politics Faculty, *The U.S. Constitution: A Reader* (Hillsdale, Michigan: Hillsdale College Press, 2015), 130.

11. Colson, *Conflict*, 483.

12. Forrest Church, *The Separation of Church and State* (Boston: Beacon Press, 2004), ix.

13. 106th Congress and 2d Session, "*What Is the Purpose of the U.S. Government?*," Our American Government (2000, Washington): 1.

14. 106th, 2d Session, "*What Is the Constitution?*," Our American Government (2000, Washington): 2.

15. Bonhoeffer, *Ethics*, 342.

16. Paul Copan and Matthew Flannagan, *Did God Really Command Genocide?* (Grand Rapids, Michigan: Baker Books, 2014), 300.

17. Colson, *Kingdoms,* 495.

18. Carl F. H. Henry, *Christian Personal Ethics* (Grand Rapids, Michigan: Baker Book house, 1979), 325.

19. Colson, *Kingdoms*, 525.

20. Church, *Church and State*, 11, 12, 14.

21. John W. Whitehead, *The Second American Revolution* (Westchester, Illinois: Crossway Books, 1982), 116.

22. Whitehead, *American Revolution*, 73.

23. Whitehead, *American Revolution*, 21.

24. Hillsdale College Faculty, *Constitution 101: The Meaning and History of the Constitution*, 2015, accessed July 4, 2017, http://online.hillsdale.edu/course/con-101.

25. Colson, *Kingdoms*, 347.

26. Copan and Flannagan, *Genocide?*, 302.

27. Ibid., 304.

28. Ibid., 300.

29. Colson, *Kingdoms*, 486.

30. Ibid., 379.

31. Ibid., 485, 486.
32. Church, *Church and State*, 30.
33. Whitehead, *American Revolution*, 31.
34. Samuel Rutherford, *Lex Rex* (Glasgow: Edinburg: M. Ogle & Son and William Collins, 1644, reprint 1843), 1, 2.
35. Church, *Church and State*, 11.
36. Church, *Church and State*, 27, 28.
37. Ibid., 344.
38. Henry, *Ethics*, 243.
39. Norman L. Geisler, *Ethics* (Grand Rapids, Michigan: Zondervan Publishing House, 1971), 192.
40. Copan and Flannagan, *Genocide?*, 303, 304.
41. Ibid., 300.
42. Henry, *Ethics*, 323.
43. Copan and Flannagan, *Genocide?*, 300.

Chapter 3

1. E.M. Blaiklock, *Tyndale New Testament Commentaries: The Acts of the Apostles*, R.V.G. Tasker, Gen Editor (Grand Rapids, Michigan: Wm. B. Eerdmanns Publishing Company, 1974), 66.
2. Blaiklock, *Tyndale, Acts*. 64.
3. Samuel Rutherford, *Lex Rex: Or, the Law and the Prince* (Glasgow: Edinburg: M. Ogle & Son and William Collins, 1843), 1.
4. R.J. Knowling, *The Expositor's Greek New Testament, Vol. 2: The Acts of the Apostles* (Grand Rapids, Michigan: Eerdmanns Publishing Company, 1983), 127.
5. F.F. Bruce, *The New International Commentary on the New Testament: The Book of Acts* (Grand Rapids, Michigan: Wm. B. Eerdmans Publishing Company, 1979), 103.
6. Bruce, *New International Commentary: Acts*, 104.
7. C.F. Keil and F. Delitzsch, *Commentary on the Old Testament*, 3 (U.S.A: Hendrikson Publishers, 1989), 429.
8. *The Pulpit Commentary: 2 Chronicles*, ed. Joseph Excell and H.D.M. Spence (Electronic Database: Hendrikson, 1990).
9. Bruce, *The New International Commentary on the New Testament: The Book of Acts*, 99.
10. R.J. Knowling, *The Expositor's Greek New Testament, Vol. 2: The Acts of the Apostles*.125.
11. Britannica.com/topic/authoritarianism, online accessed 1982, written by editors of Encyclopedia Britannica.
12. Bruce, *The New International Commentary on the New Testament: The Book of Acts*, 99.

13. Knowling, *The Expositor's, Acts*, 127.

14. Ibid, 113.

15. Charles Colson, *Kingdoms in Conflict* (Grand Rapids, Michigan: Inspirational Press, Zondervan Book House, 1987), 495.

16. John W. Whitehead, *The Second American Revolution* (Westchester, Illinois: Crossway Books, 1982), 18.

17. Lomasky, *Contract, Covenant, Constitution,* 14, 15. January 2009.

18. Ibid., 14, 15.

19. Whitehead, *American Revolution*, 29, 30.

20. Lomasky, *Contract, Covenant, Constitution*, 14, 15. January 2009.

21. Ibid, 14, 15 (as previously in CFP editing)

22. Lomasky, *Contract, Covenant, Constitution*, 16.

23. Ibid 16, 17

24. Ibid 23

25. Cornell University Law School, "Oath of Office", 5 U.S. Code 3331", Legal Information Institute

26. Whitehead, *American Revolution*, 56.

27. Ibid., 57.

28. Francis Schaeffer, *A Christian Manifesto,* (Westchester, Illinois: Crossway Books, 1981) 481

29. Whitehead, *American Revolution*, 56

30. Schaeffer, *A Christian Manifesto*, 433.

31. Kimberly Strassel, *The Dark Arts of Political Intimidation*, (n.p.: Wall Street Journal, 2016)

32. Forest Church, *The Separation of Church and State,* (Boston: Beacon Press, 2004) 27, 28

33. Schaeffer, *A Christian Manifesto,* 481

34. Colson, *Kingdoms in Conflict*, 499

35. Robert George, *Why We're Losing Liberty,* (Princeton: Princeton University, 2016)

36. David Koyzis, "Is it Time for American Citizens to Disobey Government?", Christianity Today, March 8, 2016, 2, http://www.christianitytoday.com.

Chapter 4

1. Charles Colson, *Kingdoms in Conflict* (Grand Rapids, Michigan: Zondervan Publishing House, 1987), 496, 498.

2. William Hendriksen, *New Testament Commentary*, "Exposition of the Gospel According to Mark" (Grand Rapids, Michigan: Baker Book House, 1975), 492.

3. Alexander Balmain Bruce, *The Expositor's Greek New Testament, Vol. 1, the Synoptic Gospels: Matthew*, ed. W Robertson Nicoll (Grand Rapids, Michigan: Eerdmanns, 1983), 424.

4. Colson, *Kingdoms*, 351.

5. Bruce, *The Expositor's, Matthew*, 277.

6. William L. Lane, *The New International Commentary of the New Testament*, ed. F F Bruce (Grand Rapids, Michigan: Eerdmanns, 1974), 433.

7. Hendriksen, *Mark*. 492.

8. H.E. Dana and Julius R. Mantey, "Comparative Clauses," in *A Manual Grammar for the Greek New Testament* (1955; repr., Toronto, Ontario: MacMillan Company, 1927), 275, 276.

9. Gerhard Von Rad, *Old Testament Theology*, Vol 1 (New York and Evanston: Harper Row, 1965), 370

10. Walther Eichrodt, *Theology of the Old Testament*, Vol 1 (Philadelphia: Westminster, 1959), 240.

11. Norman L. Geisler, *Ethics: Alternatives and Issues* (Grand Rapids, Michigan: Zondervan Publishing House, 1971), 180.

12. John W. Whitehead, *The Second American Revolution* (Westchester, Illinois: Crossway, 1982), 31.

13. Samuel Rutherford, *Lex Rex* (Glasgow: Edinburg: M. Ogle & Son and William Collins, 1644, Reprinted 1843), 1, 2.

14. Forrest Church, *The Separation of Church and State* (Boston: Beacon Press, 2004), 11.

15. Church, *Church and State*, 27, 28.

16. Carl F. H. Henry, *Christian Personal Ethics* (Grand Rapids, Michigan: Baker Book House, 1979), 243.

17. Geisler, *Ethics*, 181.

18. H. Brown, *Tertullian's apology; Or Defence of the Christians, against the Accusations of the Gentiles* (London: Tho. Harper, 1655), chap. 39:7.

19. C.F. Keil and F. Delitzsch, *Commentary on the Old Testament* (Peabody, Massachusetts: Hendrikson Publishers, 1989), Vol. 1, 153.

20. Ibid., 153.

21. Katheryn Pfisterer Darr, *The New Interpreter's Bible*, "Ezekiel", (Nashville: Abington Press, 2001), VI, 1,448.

22. Keil and Delitzsch, *Old Testament*, Vol. 9, 67.

23. Ralph H. Alexander, *The Expositor's Bible Commentary*, "Isaiah, Jeremiah, Lamentations, Ezekiel," ed. Frank E. Gabelein (Grand Rapids, Michigan: Zondervan, 1986), Vol 6, 904.

24. Keil and Delitzsch, *Old Testament*, Vol. 1, 409.

25. Edward P. Blair, *The Layman's Bible Commentary*, 25 (Richmond, Virginia: John Knox Press, 1964), Vol. 5, 60.

26. Keil and Delitzsch, *Commentary on the Old Testament*, Vol. 5, 402.

27. Mary Frances Owens, *The Layman's Bible Book Commentary* (Nashville: Broadman Press, 1983), 47, 48.

28. Geisler, *Ethics*, 171.

29. Barclay M. Newman Jr., *A Concise Greek-English Dictionary of the New Testament* (Stuttgart, West Germany: Wurttemberg Bible Society, 1971), 86.

30. Carl F.H. Henry, *Christian Personal Ethics*, (Grand Rapids, Michigan, Baker, 1979), 305.

31. Paul Copan and Matthew Flannagan, *Did God Really Command Genocide?* (Grand Rapids, Michigan: Baker Books, 2014), 311.

32. Geisler, *Ethics: Alternatives and Issues*, 171.

33. Copan and Flannagan, *Did God Really Command Genocide?*, 302.

34. Copan and Flannagan, *Genocide?*, 44.

35. William Barclay, *The Daily Bible Study Series*, "The Gospel of Matthew" (Philadelphia: Westminster Press, 1975), Vol. 2, 166.

36. Alexander Balmain Bruce, *Expositor's*, Matthew, 112.

37. Copan and Flannagan, *Genocide?*, 43, 47.

38. Colson, *Kingdoms*, 346.

39. Copan and Flannagan, *Genocide?*, 306.

40. Colson, *Kingdoms*, 493.

41. The United States Supreme Court, *Bowers v. Devito*, 686 F. 2d, 616, 7th Cir. accessed 1982, http://casetext.com.

42. Gary Kleck, *Targeting Guns: Firearms and Their Control* (New Jersey: Rutgers University: Transaction Publishers, 1997), 29.

43. The National Association of Chiefs of Police, "17th Annual Survey of Police Chiefs and Sheriffs," *The Police Times*, 2005, 26.

44. James D. Wright, "Armed Criminals in America: A Survey of Incarcerated Felons," *U. S. Bureau of Justice Statistics: A Federal Firearms Study* (July 1985): 30.

45. James Wright and Peter Rossi, *Armed and Dangerous: A Study of Felons and Their Firearms* (Harry Ransom Humanities Research Center; The University of Texas at Austin: Aldine, 1984), 29.

46. Geisler, *Ethics*, 194.

47. Copan and Flannagan, *Genocide?* 312.

48. Colson, *Kingdoms in Conflict*, 368.

49. Ibid., 349.

50. Ibid., 438.

51. Dietrich Bonhoeffer, *Ethics*, trans. S.C.M. Press Ltd (New York: MacMillan Company, 1955), 337.

52. Francis Schaeffer, *A Christian Manifesto* (Westchester, Illinois: Crossway Books, 1981), 425.

53. Colson, *Kingdoms*, 305.

54. Garth Lean, *Strangely Warmed* (Wheaton, Illinois: Tyndale Publishers, 1979), 62.

55. Schaeffer, *Manifesto*, 451, 452.

56. Whitehead, *American Revolution*, 163, 165.

57. Henry, *Christian Personal Ethics*, 303.

58. Geisler, *Ethics*, 179

59. Schaeffer, *Manifesto*, 424.

60. Colson, *Kingdoms*, 476.

61. Ibid., 342.

62. Neil Cole, *Organic Church: Growing Faith Where Life Happens* (San Francisco: Leadership Network, 2006), 5

63. James Hogue and Ebbie C. Smith, *Christianity Faces a Pluralistic World* (Fort Worth, Texas: Christian Literary Publications, 1989), 145.

64. Whitehead, *American Revolution*, 34.

65. Church, *Church and State*, 17, 18.

66. Church, *Church and State*, xi.

67. Bonhoeffer, *Ethics*, 347.

68. Colson, *Kingdoms*, 492.

69. Copan and Flannagan, *Genocide?*, 308.

70. John Calvin, *Institutes of the Christian Religion*, vol. 2, bk. 1 (Philadelphia: Westminster Press, 1989), 846–49.

71. Bonhoeffer, *Ethics*, 333.

72. Colson, *Kingdoms*, 352.

73. Schaeffer, *Manifesto*, 456.

74. Ibid., 482.

75. Geisler, *Ethics*, 188.

76. Colson, *Kingdoms*, 379.

77. Church, *Church and State*, 17.

78. Colson, *Kingdoms*, 344.

79. Colson, *Kingdoms*, 533.

80. Ed Silvoso, *Ekklesia* (Minneapolis, Minnesota: Chosen-Baker Publishing Group, 2017).

91. Schaeffer, *Manifesto*, 484, 485.

82. Colson, *Kingdoms*, 533.

83. Geisler, *Ethics*, 188.

84. Schaeffer, *Manifesto*, 467–74.

85. Ibid. 468, 469.

86. Colson, *Kingdoms*, 504.

87. Jay Allen Sekulow, *The Christian, the Court, the Constitution* (Virginia Beach, Virginia: American Center for Law and Justice, 2000), 28.

88. Francis Schaeffer, *The Church at the End of the Twentieth Century* (Westchester, Illinois: Crossway Books, 1982), 32.

89. Church, *Church and State*, 17.

90. Schaeffer, *Manifesto*, 491.

91. Schaeffer, *Manifesto*, 477.

92. Ibid., 474.

93. Francis Schaeffer, *Twentieth Century*, 29.

94. Charles Hodge, *Systematic Theology*, 3 vols. (Grand Rapids, Michigan: Wm. B. Eerdmanns Publishing Company, 1981), 360.

95. Colson, *Kingdoms*, 584.

96. Jonathan Kauffman, "Old Time Religion, an Evangelical Revival Is Sweeping the Nation but with Little Effect," *Wall Street Journal*, July 11, 1980, 45.

97. Rutherford, *Lex Rex*, 166–72.

98. Bonhoeffer, *Ethics*, 351.

99. Eric Metaxis, Bonhoeffer: *Pastor, Martyr, Prophet, Spy* (Nashville: Thomas Nelson, 2010), 423–31.

100. Church, *Church and State*, 14, 15.

Chapter 5

1. William Hendriksen, *New Testament Commentary: Exposition of Ephesians* (Grand Rapids, Michigan: Baker Book House, 1979), 248.

2. Walter Bauer, *A Greek-English Lexicon of the New Testament and Other Early Christian Literature*, ed. Revised and Augmented by F. Wilbur Gingrich and Frederick W. Danker, second ed. (Chicago and London: University of Chicago Press, 1957), 843.

3. Francis Foulkes, *Tyndale New Testament Commentaries*, ed. R.V.G. Tasker (Grand Rapids, Michigan: Eerdmanns Publishing Company, 1963), Vol. 10, p. 157.

4. W. Curtis Vaughn, *The Letter to the Ephesians* (Nashville: Convention Press, 1963), 115.

5. Marcus Dods, *The Expositor's Greek Testament: The Epistle to the Hebrews*, ed. W. Robertson Nicoll (Grand Rapids, Michigan: Wm. B. Eerdmanns Publishing Company, 1983), Vol. 4, pp. 378–79.

6. Foy Valentine, *The Layman's Bible Book* Commentary: Hebrews, James, 1 & 2 Peter (Nashville: Broadman Press, 1981), 64.

7. Dietrich Bonhoeffer, *Ethics*, s. c. m. press, ltd. translation ed. (New York: MacMillan Company, 1955), 342.

8. John Calvin, *Institutes of the Christian Religion* (Philadelphia: Westminster Press, 1910), 2:1487.

9. Whitehead, John, *The Second American Revolution* (Westchester, Illinois: Crossway Books, 1982), 21.

10. Francis Schaeffer, *A Christian Manifesto* (Westchester, Illinois: Crossway Books, 1981), 430.

11. Charles W. Colson, *Kingdoms in Conflict* (Grand Rapids, Michigan: Zondervan Publishing House, 1987), 368.

12. Schaeffer, *A Christian Manifesto*, 485, 486.

13. Jacques Ellul, *The Presence of the Kingdom* (New York: Seabury Press, 1967), 47.

14. Colson, *Kingdoms*, 371.

15. *The U. S. Constitution*, ed. Hillsdale College Politics Faculty (Hillsdale, Michigan: Hillsdale College Press, 2015), 130, 131.

16. Forrest Church, *The Separation of Church and State* (Boston: Beacon Press, 2004), vii, 19.

17. The Westminster Assembly, *The Westminster Confession of Faith* (Carlisle, Pennsylvania: Banner of Truth Press, Broadcast in 1647), XX, 2.

18. Bonhoeffer, *Ethics*, 347, 349.

Chapter 6

1. Russell Moore, *Onward* (Nashville, Tennessee: B & H Books, 2015), 49.

2. Ibid., 66, 67.

3. Paul Copan and Matthew Flannagan, *Did God Really Command Genocide?* (Grand Rapids, Michigan: Baker Books, 2014), 44.

4. John Jefferson Davis, *Evangelical Ethics: Issues Facing the Church Today* (Phillipsburg: P&R Publishing, 2015), 239.

5. *Tucker Carlson Tonight*, "Witches Cast Spells on "Wicked" Trump," Fox News, September 19, 2017, 5:01 PM.

6. Larry F. Johnston, "At the Crossroads," *Christian Research Institute: Life and Truth Matter* (August 2017): 1, 5, http://www.equip.org.

7. Garth Lean, *Strangely Warmed* (Wheaton, Illinois: Tyndale Publishers, 1979), 62.

8. Johnston, "*At the Crossroads*," 5.

9. Walter Bauer, *A Greek-English Lexicon of the New Testament and Other Early Christian Literature*, ed. Revised Danker and Augmented by F. Wilbur Gingrich and Frederick W., second ed. (Chicago and London: University of Chicago Press, 1957), 27, 28.

10. John W. Whitehead, *The Second American Revolution* (Westchester, Illinois: Crossway Books, 1982), 162.

11. George Barna, *America at the Crossroads: Explosive Trends Shaping America's Future* (Grand Rapids, Michigan: Baker Books, 2016), 36.

12. Penny Lea, *Sing a Little Louder*, accessed August 27, 2017, Abstract retrieved from http://www.internationalwallofprayer.org/A-010-Holocaust-Memorial-Day-Stover.html.

13. Francis Schaeffer, *The Church at the End of the Twentieth Century* (Westchester, Illinois: Crossway Books, 1970), 29, 20.

14. Russell Moore, *Onward: Engaging the Culture without Losing the Gospel* (Nashville, Tennessee: B & H Publishing Group, 2015), 222.

15. Cliff Daugherty, "*Quest Institute Quality Education Center*," 27th Annual Transform our World Global Conference. October 12, 2017.

16. Ed Silvoso, *Ekklesia: Rediscovering God's Instrument for Global Transformation* (Minneapolis, Minnesota: Baker Publishing Group-Chosen, 2017), 180.

About the Author

Dr. Louis Day has been both a successful pastor and business entrepreneur for over twenty-five years. He has been blessed to travel across the world in ministry and business. Having earned his Master of Divinity and Doctor of Philosophy degrees, his passion is to awaken the Church from her "Churchianity" and to remind them that they are the people of God who are a force to be reckoned with.

Currently living in Colorado, Louis teaches concealed-weapon training and instructs mass shooter event confrontation for Churches, schools, and hospitals. He and his wife have raised six children who have grown to have thriving families of their own across America and beyond.